"The topic of this book speaks to my heart and will serve well everyone who reads it."

—HORST SCHULZE, cofounder of Ritz-Carlton and author
of *Excellence Wins*

"When I started my nonprofit, there were a million ideas swirling around, and a wise humanitarian encouraged me to deeply focus on one thing. That one thing was water, and that encouragement began a movement that's helped ten million people across the globe get clean water. Jordan Raynor gives the same advice in this book, showing you precisely how to find and focus on your one thing."

—SCOTT HARRISON, founder and CEO of charity: water
and *New York Times* best-selling author of *Thirst*

"In *Master of One,* Jordan Raynor uses real-life examples to point the way to a satisfied life, one of purpose, meaning, and happiness."

—SHERRON WATKINS, Enron whistle-blower and *Time*
magazine's 2002 Person of the Year

"Christians ought to have the highest standards for excellence in our work. That's the heart of this book, and I am so grateful Jordan has written it."

—BOBBY BOWDEN, second-winningest coach in Division 1 college
football history

"Jordan Raynor writes with a clear and powerful conviction—the path to exceptional work is not about more work but about better work. Excellence is waiting for us if we will just dig in."

—CAREY NIEUWHOF, founding pastor of Connexus Church

"My stepfather, C. S. Lewis, used to say, 'We do not need more people writing Christian books. What we need is more Christians writing good books.' This is true for any Christian in any line of work. I am thrilled that Jordan Raynor has taken the time to explore this idea more fully in *Master of One*."

—DOUGLAS GRESHAM, stepson of C. S. Lewis and executive producer of Disney's and Netflix's *Chronicles of Narnia* films

"Both social science and God's Word refute the conventional wisdom that simply following your passions will lead to the ultimate satisfaction of vocation. In *Master of One*, Jordan Raynor articulately argues that we find true vocational happiness when we focus first on bringing joy to God and others by doing our work masterfully well."

—MISSY WALLACE, executive director of the Nashville Institute for Faith and Work

"Work is an opportunity to serve the world. But if we are to serve well, we ought to have the highest standards of excellence in our work. This book will help you find and focus on the work you can do most masterfully well."

—JEFF GOINS, best-selling author of *The Art of Work* and *Real Artists Don't Starve*

"Jordan Raynor does an awesome job communicating how the gospel impacts our work—especially the work of the entrepreneur and culture maker."

—HENRY KAESTNER, cofounder of Bandwidth and founder of Faith Driven Entrepreneur

"Jordan Raynor is definitely speaking to me when thinking about the master multitasker. I already have joy for living life for an audience of one, but I can't wait to learn the principles to find focus and precision within my life."

—TAMIKA CATCHINGS, four-time Olympic gold medalist, ten-time WNBA All-Star, and former WNBA MVP

"Serve the world by picking a lane and getting masterfully good at your craft. This book will show you how."

—Chris Graebe, host of the *StartupCamp* podcast

"I loved *Master of One*! Jordan's writing frees you from the paralysis of indecisiveness and provides a simple framework for choosing the work you will do most masterfully well for the glory of God."

—Stefan Kunz, letterer, designer, and illustrator behind @stefankunz on Instagram and YouTube

"Jordan Raynor offers a practical guide to finding and focusing on the work you can do most exceptionally well—not for your own sake but to bring benefit to the world. We need this message right now. And the great news is that this book exhibits what it teaches: it is a book on mastery that is masterfully written."

—Matt Perman, director of career development at the King's College, New York City, and author of *What's Best Next*

Find and Focus on the
Work You Were Created to Do

MASTER *of* ONE

Jordan Raynor

Best-Selling Author of *Called to Create*

WATERBROOK

Master of One

Hardcover ISBN 978-0-525-65333-2
eBook ISBN 978-0-525-65334-9

Library of Congress Cataloging-in-Publication Data
Names: Raynor, Jordan, 1986– author.
Title: Master of one : find and focus on the work you were created to do / Jordan Raynor.
Description: First Edition. | Colorado Springs : WaterBrook, 2020. | Includes bibliographical references.
Identifiers: LCCN 2019012692 | ISBN 9780525653332 (hardcover) | ISBN 9780525653349 (electronic)
Subjects: LCSH: Vocation—Christianity. | Excellence—Religious aspects—Christianity.
Classification: LCC BV4740 .R39 2020 | DDC 248.8/8—dc23
LC record available at https://lccn.loc.gov/2019012692

Printed in Canada
2020—First Edition

10 9 8 7 6 5 4 3 2 1

To Kara, whose loving sacrifice
allows me to pursue mastery of the
work the Father has created me to do.

Contents

Introduction xi

PART I: THE PURPOSE *of* MASTERY

Chapter 1: Excellence in All Things 3

Chapter 2: Proclaiming the Excellencies of God 21

Chapter 3: The Ministry of Excellence 39

PART II: THE PATH *to* MASTERY

Chapter 4: Start with "The One" in Mind 57

Chapter 5: Explore 77

Chapter 6: Choose 97

Chapter 7: Eliminate 117

Chapter 8: Master 135

PART III: THE PROMISE *of* MASTERY

Chapter 9: Salt and Light 157

Chapter 10: The Room Where It Happens 175

Chapter 11: Share the Master's Happiness 189

Acknowledgments 201

Notes 205

Introduction

There's an old saying that goes, "He's a jack-of-all-trades and a master of none," used to describe someone who is good at many different things but not excellent at any one of them. Early in my career this described me perfectly. By the time I was twenty-five, I had already had nearly a dozen jobs, including working in a call center, playing piano for tips, selling newspapers, working for a tech startup, starting and selling my own tech startup, running a political campaign, and interning at the White House. Along the way I picked up a diverse set of skills that helped me achieve a reasonable level of success and a more-than-healthy dose of self-confidence.

But one of my mentors and personal heroes was about to cut me down to size. Sitting across the table at lunch was Rick Mortensen, a master of one craft, whose career looked quite different from mine. Rick had spent nearly three decades building an incredibly successful civil engineering practice. It seemed like everyone in the community knew and respected Rick due to his excellent work and that of his firm. But Rick wasn't just excellent at the office; he was also an excellent husband, father, and follower of Jesus Christ. Rick was the real deal, and every time he agreed to have lunch with me, I tried to soak in as much wisdom as I could.

The topic of conversation at this particular lunch was my career. I was considering leaving the company that had bought my first startup, and I wanted Rick's advice on the next professional move I should make. As I reminded him of the winding road my career had taken up to that point, he leaned forward and asked me a question I'll never forget: "Jordan, what is the one thing you want to *really* sink your teeth into?" The question caught me off guard. *One thing?* I repeated in my head. The question seemed unanswerable. There were *so* many things I wanted to do in my work. How in the world could I choose just one to focus on?

While Rick was too gracious to say it, he was pointing out that I was a jack-of-all-trades and a master of none. While it pained me to admit it, he was right. I had yet to find "my thing" that I was prepared to go big on, or in the words of my mentor, to "sink my teeth into." But as the weeks and months after that lunch went by, I realized Rick was asking an essential question that I had to answer for myself.

MASTERS *of* NONE

I don't think my story is unique. In fact, I think it is more common now than ever before. Perhaps the most significant research ever conducted on the topic of excellence in the workplace was completed by Dr. Anders Ericsson, who found that in order to achieve mastery in any field, one must spend roughly ten thousand hours purposefully practicing that skill.[1] *Ten thousand hours!* To put that in perspective, let's do some quick math. Let's assume that you work an average of fifty hours per week, and you spend twenty of those fifty hours checking email and responding to the seemingly endless inbound requests that demand your attention. That leaves you with thirty hours a week to work on the particular skill you are seeking to master. Even if you were somehow able to lock yourself in a room and never take another meeting or call again, it would still take you more than *six years* to achieve mastery.

Given the way we work today, it's no wonder we are a society of jacks-and-jills-of-all-trades and masters of none. A recent study found that 21 percent of millennials reported changing jobs in the last year.[2] Another study found that this most recent generation of workers will change jobs four times in their first decade out of college.[3] But perhaps the most significant trend in our society's move away from mastery is the rise of the "gig economy" with people of all ages trading in traditional full-time employment for a smorgasbord of different part-time jobs. Some experts estimate that more than 40 percent of the American workforce will be independent contractors by the time this book is in your hands![4]

But this is not a book about the gig economy, and I'm not trying to make you feel guilty about hopping from job to job. Trust me, I am the *last* person who can criticize professional exploration. (My average tenure in any given endeavor is roughly two years.) I cite the research above to make a point I think we all intuitively know to be true: many of us are making "a millimeter of progress in a million directions" with our lives and our careers.[5] We are good at a lot of

> **We are overcommitted, overwhelmed, and overstressed, spending way too much time focused on minutiae rather than the work we believe God created us to do.**

different things, but we aren't excellent, masterful, or exceptional at any one of them. We are overcommitted, overwhelmed, and overstressed, spending way too much time focused on minutiae rather than the work we believe God created us to do.

As you will see later in this book, being a jack-of-all-trades is not bad in and of itself. Most of the time it is simply a good and inevitable by-product of exploring our calling. But the idea of being described as a mediocre "master of none" should make us Christians sick to our stomachs. Why? Because mediocre work fails to accomplish the essence of the Christian life: to serve others and to glorify God.

You and I are called to be image bearers of the exceptional God. In Ephesians 5:1, Paul instructs the church "as beloved children" to "be imitators of God" (ESV). Commenting on this passage, theologian Andreas Köstenberger writes, "How should we respond to God's excellence? In short, we should seek to imitate and emulate it. . . . As God's redeemed children, we are to strive to be like God. This, it appears, includes striving for excellence."[6] John Piper put it this way: "God created me—and you—to live with a single, all-embracing, all-transforming passion—namely, a passion to glorify God by enjoying and displaying his supreme excellence in all the spheres of life."[7] Are we as the church doing such masterful work that the world can see the "supreme excellence" of the Father shining through his children? Or are we masters of none, doing mediocre or perhaps even good work but little that's excellent enough to make the world take notice of the exceptional God we serve?

One of my favorite descriptions of Jesus comes from Mark 7:37: "People were overwhelmed with amazement. 'He [Jesus] has done everything well.'" As followers of Christ we are to seek to imitate Jesus in every way imaginable. Can we honestly say we are doing *everything* well? Can we say we are doing *anything* masterfully well?

When we are stretched as thin as most of us are today, we are all but guaranteed to do everything with mediocrity rather than mastery. As Köstenberger pointed out, "This mediocrity has in many cases become a curse—a curse that has kept us from reaching our personal, creative, and [professional] potential given to us by God, and has prevented us from impacting other believers as well as unbelievers for the glory of God and for his kingdom."[8]

Years ago, Franky Schaeffer summarized this idea in a book titled *Addicted to Mediocrity*. While I agree with much of what Schaeffer says in that volume, I take issue with the idea that it is mediocrity to which we are addicted. Nobody enjoys feeling as if they are doing shoddy work. We all yearn to be masters of a craft. But we *are* addicted to something else that leads to mediocrity: the idea of more. For too long we have believed the lie that more activity, more roles, and more responsibility equals greater effectiveness. As this book will show, nothing could be further from the truth. The path to doing our best work for God's glory and the good of others is the path of "less but better."[9]

So, in a world with unprecedented flexibility and a number of options for our work, how do we avoid becoming masters of none? How do we find the work we can do most exceptionally well in service of God and others? What is the solution to being a jack-of-all-trades and a master of none? The solution is becoming a *master of one*.

MASTERS OF ONE

While you're likely familiar with the phrase "jack-of-all-trades, master of none," you may not know that the saying is rumored to be a misquote of Benjamin Franklin, who supposedly encouraged his readers to be a "Jack of all trades, and a master of *one*."[10] It appears that Franklin was making an entirely different point than how the phrase is understood today. He was saying that, while it is good to be well-rounded and have a wide variety of interests, skills, and hobbies, there ought to be one thing that we go big on, that we sink our teeth into, that we pursue mastery of.

Whether or not Franklin was the one to utter this phrase is irrelevant. The fact is that in order to best glorify God and love others through our vocations, we must do our work with excellence. And we can't do our most excellent work until we discern the work God has created us to do most exceptionally well, and then, once we've found it, focus on becoming a master of that craft. Throughout this book I will build a case around this core idea, leaning heavily on God's Word, extensive research of the world's best business and scientific literature, my own personal experiences, and the stories of more than twenty Christians who are undeniable masters of one vocational thing. I am confident you will walk away after reading this book convinced of what so many others have come to hold as a central truth of life: the path to making the greatest impact through our work is the path of less but better, of continually pruning our careers in order to focus on the work we were created to do most exceptionally well for the glory of God and the good of others.

Except for God's Word, perhaps no book has influenced this one more than Greg McKeown's *Essentialism: The Disciplined Pursuit of Less.* In it, McKeown said, "When individuals are involved in too many disparate activities—even good activities—they can fail to achieve their essential mission."[11] I don't think anybody in history understood this better than Jesus himself. Even though the Son of God was omnipotent—fully God *and* fully man—he still displayed a remarkable understanding of the natural limits time and attention place on our ability to fulfill our "essential mission," or what Jesus referred to as the work the Father gave him to do (see John 17:4).

In the gospel of Luke, we are told, "As the time approached for him to be taken up to heaven, Jesus resolutely set out for Jerusalem" (Luke 9:51). Another translation says that Jesus "set his face to go to Jerusalem." The picture here isn't one of Jesus scattering himself across a myriad of nonessential activities. Jesus was laser focused on his one thing: preaching the good news of redemption in word and in deed from Galilee to Judea and ultimately to a cross in Jerusalem. Along the way to fulfilling that mission, Jesus stopped by the home of Mary and Martha in what has become a legendary biblical account. As Luke shared:

> As Jesus and his disciples were on their way, he came to a village where a woman named Martha opened her home to him. She had a sister called Mary, who sat at the Lord's feet listening to what he said. But Martha was distracted by all the preparations that had to be made. She came to him and asked, "Lord, don't you care that my sister has left me to do the work by myself? Tell her to help me!"
>
> "Martha, Martha," the Lord answered, "you are worried and upset about many things, but few things are needed—or indeed only one. Mary has chosen what is better, and it will not be taken away from her." (10:38–42)

Jesus had the mind-set of an essentialist on his way to fulfilling the one thing the Father called him to do, and here he is teaching Mary and Martha to do the same. In that moment the one essential thing was not cooking another dish or cleaning up the house—it was sitting at the feet of Jesus. Commenting on this passage, Pastor Timothy Keller hit the nail on the head: "[Mary] decided what was important, and she did not let the day-to-day get her away from that. As a result, she was drawn into a greatness we don't even dream of. Because we are more like Martha than Mary, we're sinking in a sea of mediocrity."[12]

The world is constantly pressuring us to be more like Martha than

Mary, convincing us that the path to happiness and impact is the path of more—more jobs, more skills, more responsibility, more information, more fun, and more money. But here Jesus offers us a better, simpler, saner way. He offers us the path of less but better: *"Few things are needed . . . indeed only one."* In a world full of Marthas, let us allow Jesus's words to permeate every aspect of our lives, especially our work. Instead of scattering our gifts and energy in a million different directions, let us seek the one vocational thing we believe the Father has given us to do and then master that work for his glory and the good of others.

A Guide to This Book

In my previous book *Called to Create,* I make the case that our work is one of the primary ways we reveal God's character to the world and love and serve our neighbors as ourselves. This book builds upon that theme, helping you find, focus on, and master the work God has created you to do most exceptionally well.

I've divided the book into three parts. In part 1 we will dig deeper into "The Purpose of Mastery," a topic we have just begun to explore. These first three chapters will continue making the case that, as Christians, we ought to have the highest standards for excellence in our work and that the strategy for producing exceptional work is to master one vocational thing at a time. In chapter 1, NFL Hall of Fame coach Tony Dungy will help us understand the biblical mandate for "excellence in all things" and how that mandate forces us to be incredibly focused in our work. In chapter 2 we will see how masterful work can proclaim the excellencies of God by visiting la Sagrada Família in Barcelona, Spain, the world's largest church, and by getting to know an

Olympic gold medalist before and after his salvation. Finally, in chapter 3, you will meet a neonatal intensive care unit nurse and the National Basketball Association's first black female CEO, both of whom demonstrate how focused, excellent work is necessary to love our neighbors as ourselves.

Part 2 is the longest and most practical section of the book. In it we will walk together along "The Path to Mastery": a biblical approach to finding and focusing on the one thing God has created you to do most exceptionally well in your work. This is a process so nuanced that it can't be reduced to a one-size-fits-all formula. However, through my extensive research and interviews, I have uncovered clear themes that will help you discover and master the work God has called you to do. In chapter 4 we will define what we're looking for in our "one thing" and make the important distinction that our chosen area of focus can be specific or quite broad, as in the case of C. S. Lewis, who applied his one masterful skill of teaching in many different contexts. Then, with a clear picture of what it is we are looking for in our one thing, we will spend chapters 5 through 8 walking down the path to mastery together, with each chapter dedicated to one of the four steps: Explore, Choose, Eliminate, and Master. In this part of the book, we will answer questions such as:

- What is the quickest path to experimenting with and choosing your one vocational thing?
- How do you know when you've found your one thing or, in other words, your calling?
- Is a calling something you choose or something that chooses you?
- Once you've said yes to your one thing, how do you practically say no to everything else?

- How do you get masterful at something if you can't find
  the right mentor?
- What are the keys to mastery that separate masters from
  their less masterful counterparts?

To help answer these questions, you will read compelling stories of
masters you may know (such as Fred Rogers, Chip and Joanna Gaines,
Emily Ley, and charity: water's Scott Harrison) and many you likely
don't know (including a teacher, a pilot, and a social entrepreneur).

Finally, in part 3 you will hear inspiring stories that illustrate "The
Promise of Mastery." In chapter 9 you will hear from Lecrae, Andrew
Stanton (director of *Stranger Things* and *Finding Nemo*), and Douglas
Gresham (producer of *Chronicles of Narnia* films), who make a compelling case that masterful work helps Christians fulfill their role as salt
and light (see Matthew 5:13–15). In chapter 10 you will meet masters
who have leveraged their power for the good of others, including Sherron Watkins, a Christ follower who, through her excellent work as an
accountant at Enron Corporation, was in a position to help bring down
one of the largest and most corrupt companies in US history. Finally, in
chapter 11 we will unpack the biblical promise that when we pursue
masterful work as a means of glorifying God and serving others, we are
invited to share in our heavenly Master's happiness.

Throughout this book (and especially in part 2), you will likely find
yourself wanting a more hands-on tool as you seek to find, focus on,
and master your one vocational thing. To facilitate this I have developed a free "Master of One Notebook," filled with practical prompts,
additional resources, and plenty of space for you to work out how the
ideas in this book apply to your own work. This is also a great tool to
help you work through the concepts of this book with a small group. To
download the free notebook, visit jordanraynor.com/MOO.

Your One Thing

In the months and years after that lunch with my mentor Rick, his question stayed tucked away in the back of my mind: *"What is the one thing you want to really sink your teeth into?"* Through many years of trials and failures, prayers and pivots, the Lord made it clear to me what my one thing is: I am an entrepreneur, skilled in the art of taking calculated risks to create new things for the good of others.

While my one thing is fairly broad, I apply it with an ever-increasing amount of focus. When I started writing this book, I was applying my skills as an entrepreneur to just two projects: writing books like this one and running the venture-backed tech startup, Threshold 360,

> **The path to doing our most exceptional work is the path of less but better.**

as its CEO. Through tremendous personal sacrifice, I was able to fulfill both of those roles with excellence for a while; but as this book began to take shape, I became so convinced of its core thesis that I decided to do what many people told me was crazy—I replaced myself as CEO of Threshold in order to focus all my professional energy on creating products like the one you hold in your hand. That was the most difficult decision I've ever made professionally. And while it required me to leave a team I love (and a relatively stable income), I'm totally convinced the decision was necessary. Why? Because I've learned what I believe you will be convinced of by the end of this book: the path to doing our most exceptional work is the path of less but better. It's not about filling up your calendar or spreading yourself so thin that you can't possibly fulfill your commitments with any degree of excellence. You achieve true mastery when you identify the few things God has created you to do most exceptionally well and work at them "with all your heart, as working for the Lord" (Colossians 3:23).

Maybe you're at a turning point in your career but you have no idea where God is calling you next. Maybe you're doing work today that you believe to be "your thing," but you're looking for a fresh perspective on the topic of vocation. Or maybe you committed to your one professional thing years ago, and you are looking to better understand what you can do to become a world-class master of your craft. Wherever you are on the path to mastery, this book is for you. I pray the Lord uses this book to build stronger conviction about the work he has called you to do and that you walk away with a treasure trove of practical wisdom to help you do more exceptional work for the glory of God and the good of others.

Let's begin!

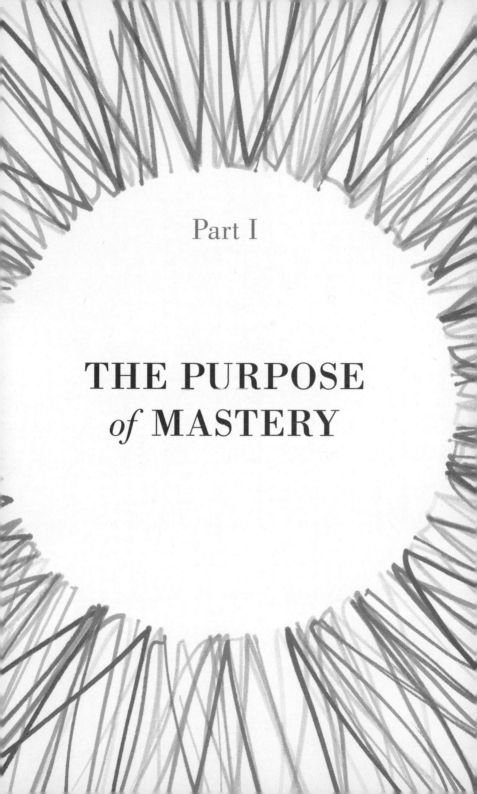

Part I

THE PURPOSE
of MASTERY

Chapter 1

Excellence in All Things

Whether you eat or drink or whatever you do, do it all for the glory of God.

1 Corinthians 10:31

There's no denying that Tony Dungy was a master of his craft. During his twenty-eight-year career, Dungy rose to become one of the most successful and beloved coaches in the history of the National Football League. In his first job as a head coach, Dungy did the seemingly impossible by turning the perennially pathetic Tampa Bay Buccaneers into a playoff-bound powerhouse. Then, after a move to Indianapolis, Dungy led the Colts to their first Super Bowl victory in thirty-six years, making Dungy the first African American head coach to ever hoist the Vince Lombardi Trophy.

As anyone close to Dungy will tell you, the soft-spoken coach is intensely passionate about the pursuit of excellence, holding the highest standards for himself and his players. But what inspired Dungy to work with such a passion for exceptionalism? Much like the other masters throughout this book, Dungy's motivation for excellence in his work stemmed from something much deeper, more sustainable, and more God honoring than the pursuit of fame, fortune, and trophies. Dungy was inspired by his parents—both of whom were masterful educators—to pursue excellence as a means of glorifying God and serving others. Remembering his parents' example, Dungy said, "My parents were definitions of excellence in teaching. It was important to them to be the best that they could be—not for personal reasons, but that was their concept of serving. They wanted to serve people in the best way possible."[1]

That commitment to mastery had a lasting impact on Dungy, who has thought a lot about excellence throughout his career. "Excellence is doing something at the very highest level it can be done using all your capabilities and everything God has given you," Dungy said. "I talk about excellence a lot, because I think from a Christian perspective, that can get lost sometimes. . . . We don't always think of excellence as a Christian concept, but I think God does desire us to be excellent at what we do. . . . Just because we're Christians doesn't mean we should take the approach to just move forward and let the Lord handle it. . . . He wants us to be excellent in what we do. He's placed us in our careers. . . . We do have a responsibility to be the very best we can be in whatever field we decide to take up. We all run to receive a prize and to win. I never want to forget that part of it. We should run to win."[2]

Throughout his career, Dungy won a lot. If there was ever a doubt that Dungy was a master of his craft as a coach, his induction into the NFL's Pro Football Hall of Fame certainly removed that skepticism. As Dungy took the stage in Canton, Ohio, to receive the Ring of Excellence, the audience of adoring fans, family, and former players erupted in rapturous applause. Clearly these fans were celebrating Dungy's excellence on the field. But as anyone who knows Dungy will tell you, they were applauding something much more; they were celebrating a man who understands that, while he is called to be excellent in his work, his faith commands him to be excellent in *all* things, including as a husband and father.

In a moving speech, Marvin Harrison (Dungy's former player and fellow Hall of Fame inductee) addressed his former coach directly, saying, "Coach Dungy. My final head coach. I could sit up here for . . . fifteen minutes and tell you about how important it was to have you as my coach and talk about football. But what you brought to our team and to me was more important than anything. You taught us how to be teammates. You taught us how to be men. But the most important thing is you taught us about fatherhood. . . . So, I want to thank you for that."[3]

Harrison's sentiment has been echoed by countless players Dungy has coached and mentored throughout his career. But Dungy didn't just tell others how to be an excellent father; he modeled it. I grew up in Tampa Bay, and I still remember seeing Dungy with his kids at sporting events where my friends and I were playing. Even at the height of his career, Dungy always seemed to make the time to cheer his kids on from the sidelines.

"If you're only focused on excellence in your job or excellence on the field, you will get totally out of balance and out of whack," Dungy said. "Yes, I need to be excellent as a coach. I need to be excellent as a Christian. I need to be excellent as a father. I need to be excellent as a person in the community and strive for that excellence everywhere and not just in one area."[4]

Dungy's comments bring to mind the motto of the late, great pastor, Dr. D. James Kennedy, who encouraged his congregation to pursue "excellence in all things and all things to God's glory."[5] While this book is primarily about excellence in your chosen work, Kennedy and Dungy remind us of a biblical truth that is critical to understand before we progress past this first chapter: As Christians, God has

> **It is precisely because we are called to be excellent in all things that we can't commit to being excellent at many things.**

called us to be excellent in *all* things, not just in our chosen vocation. 1 Corinthians 10:31 makes clear the standard we are called to: "Whether you eat or drink or whatever you do, do it all for the glory of God." In *whatever* we do, we are to do it *all* for the glory of God, never settling for anything short of excellence.

Glorify is a word we throw around so much in Christian circles that it has become tragically difficult to define. In fact, one of the most highlighted passages in the Kindle edition of my previous book is John Piper's definition of *glorify*. Since so many people found that definition helpful, allow me to reintroduce it here. According to Piper, "'Glorifying' means feeling and thinking and acting in ways that *reflect his greatness,* that make much of God, that give evidence of the supreme greatness of all his attributes and the all-satisfying beauty of his manifold perfections" (emphasis added).[6]

You and I are called to reflect God's greatness and imitate his character to the world. This is the very essence of what it means to glorify God. But what is his character? Scripture describes God in many ways, but it is his character of excellence that is perhaps most visible to us. So, when Scripture commands that in "whatever you do," you "do it all for the glory of God," we are being called to the passionate pursuit of excellence in whatever we commit ourselves to.

All of us have been called to multiple roles in life. We have been called to be excellent wives and husbands, mothers and fathers, daughters and sons, friends and church members. If we are going to fulfill all these callings with excellence while also pursuing excellence in our chosen work, it is going to require a tremendous amount of focus in our careers. Again, recall Dr. Anders Ericsson's study, which states that mastery of any vocation requires roughly ten thousand hours of "purposeful practice." The reality is that excellence requires an unusual amount of hard work and dedication. Given this, and the many things outside our careers that God has called us to be excellent in, there is simply no way we can pursue mastery at many things professionally at the same time. It defies the laws of science and time. It is precisely because we are called to be excellent in all things that we can't commit to being excellent at many things.

You and I have a choice to be either a master of none or a master of one. We must pick a path. The path to excellence in our work is the path of singularity. If we want to make our greatest contribution to the world for the glory of God and the good of others, we are going to have to adopt the mind-set of a craftsperson and get really focused and insanely good at the thing God has put us on this earth to do.

> **The path to excellence in our work is the path of singularity.**

If you are still harboring some resistance to this idea that the path to excellence is the path of less but better, I'm willing to bet that you have been a victim of being sold one (or more) of three lies about work and calling that are so pervasive today they often go unchecked. If we are to pursue excellence in all things for the glory of God and the good of others, we need to challenge the following conventional wisdom and replace these lies with biblical truths.

Lie #1: You Can Be Anything You Want to Be

John Mark Comer would love to have been a professional basketball player. As a kid, he loved watching *Pistol Pete,* the classic movie about Pete Maravich who, through years of practice, grew to become a basketball great. Comer dreamed of living a similar story and eventually playing for the National Basketball Association (NBA). "There was just one problem," Comer said. "I *suck* at basketball. I mean, I'm really, *really* bad at it. It took me a while to figure that out, and then I had to go bury the dream in my backyard, along with my ball and jersey. It was a sad day."[7]

Today, Comer is the teaching pastor at Bridgetown Church in Portland, Oregon. He's also one of my favorite authors.* One of the things I love about Comer is that he is super clear about the work God has called him to master. "Usually God's calling is a short list—just a few things," Comer said. "In my case, I'm called to lead my church, teach the Scriptures, and bring my family along for the ride. That's what I'm saying yes to."[8]

But while Comer is clear on his mission, he empathizes with others still searching for the work God has created them to do. This is largely due to Comer's recognition that for way too long we have been sold the pervasive lie that we can be anything we want to be. "I was brought up in a culture that essentially said, John Mark, you can do anything you put your mind to," Comer said. "If you work hard enough, if you believe in yourself, if you're patient, you can do anything. This is *such* a middle-class-and-above American way to think. Nobody in the developing world would ever talk like that. . . . But . . . this idea of 'I can be anything I want' is bred into us by our ancestry. And it's not all bad. It gave me the courage to dream and ideate and step out in life. But it's also dangerous because, sadly, *it's not true.* I *can't* be anything I want to be, no matter how hard I work or how much I believe in myself. All I can be is *me.* Who the Creator made John Mark to be."[9]

Comer hits the nail on the head, expounding upon a truth that is embedded deeply in Scripture: God has created each of us uniquely, with particular passions and gifts. The Bible doesn't portray God as

---

* Seriously, if you have yet to read Comer's *Garden City,* put this book down and go read that.

some manager of a cosmic manufacturing plant, pushing a button and sitting back to watch the production of millions of homogenous humans. No, all throughout Scripture, the biblical authors use beautiful language to portray God as an intentional craftsman, putting time and great care into the design of each unique human being. Consider the following verses (emphasis added):

> Before I *formed you* in the womb I knew you, before you
> were born I set you apart. (Jeremiah 1:5)

> Your hands *shaped me* and *made me.* Will you now turn
> and destroy me? Remember that you *molded me* like clay.
> (Job 10:8–9)

> For you created my inmost being; you *knit me* together
> in my mother's womb. (Psalm 139:13)

You get the point. God has meticulously designed each one of us. As the apostle Paul tells us in Romans 12:6, this includes God's granting of "different gifts, according to the grace given to each of us." God created you and me with a unique mix of passions and talents, and he has called us to steward those gifts well. In other words, there are certain kinds of work that God has designed us to do exceptionally well and, naturally, other kinds of work at which we are unlikely to excel.

But haven't technology, access to information, and economic prosperity made it possible for us to choose to do nearly any work imaginable? No doubt. We are living at a time when we have an unprecedented number of options for our work. Now more than ever we have the ability to choose virtually any career we want. However, just because we have more options doesn't mean we can do everything with excellence.

Pretend for a second that you have decided you want your car to be a boat. You live near a lake and have the option to drive your car into the water; but if you do, you aren't going to get very far. Your car may be an excellent car, but it is never going to be an exceptional boat. Why? Because your car was designed to be a car, not a boat.

The same is true for you and me in our careers. Yes, you can choose to be anything you want to be. But if our mandate is "excellence in all things and all things for God's glory," we would be wise to understand how God has created us and choose work that aligns with his design, ensuring that we make our greatest possible contribution to the world. If we choose work that is out of line with the gifts God has given us, we may be temporarily satisfied, but we won't be on the path to mastery, with the potential to become the very best versions of ourselves for the sake of God's glory and the good of others.

No matter how hard John Mark Comer tries, he's never going to play basketball in the NBA. He may enjoy shooting hoops in the front yard with his kids, but basketball is never going to be the one thing that Comer does masterfully well. In the words of the old US Army slogan, we can only "Be all we can be." You and I aren't called to "Be all we *want* to be" or "Be all we *choose* to be." We are called to be the most excellent versions of who God has *created* us to be. Comer put this well when he said, "Our job isn't to fit into some mold or prove something to the world; it's to unlock who God's made us to be, and then go be it."[10]

The lie that we can be anything we want to be is particularly dangerous because it paves the way to a second, more subtle lie that so many of us have fallen for.

Lie #2: You Can Do Everything You Want to Do

Lounging in the living room of our townhouse in Tallahassee, I declared to my college roommates that I wanted to move to Nashville to be a songwriter.

"Of course you do," my roommate Ryan said, rolling his eyes as he hopped off the couch and exited the room. When he returned, Ryan was carrying a pen and a pad of paper. "Okay, let's make a list of everything you've ever said you wanted to do." It took almost no time for my roommates and me to fill the page with a long and diverse list of my ambitions, which included (but were certainly not limited to) president of the United States, Oscar-winning composer, cast member of a Broadway musical, best-selling author, flight attendant, cruise ship piano player, speechwriter, Josh Lyman from *The West Wing*, and television producer.

"You're going to need nine lives to accomplish half of this," Ryan said. The comment made in jest illustrates a more serious point: when we adopt the lie that we can be anything we want to be, we can easily fall for the tangential lie that we can do everything we want to do, ignoring the laws of time and trade-offs. In his book *Essentialism*, Greg McKeown put it this way: "The idea that we can have it all and do it all is not new. This myth has been peddled for so long, I believe virtually everyone alive today is infected with it. It is sold in advertising. It is championed in corporations. It is embedded in job descriptions that provide huge lists of required skills and experience as standard. It is embedded in university applications that require dozens of extracurricular activities. What *is* new is how especially damaging this myth is today, in a time when choice and expectations have increased exponentially."[11]

The truth is, you can't "do it all" so long as you accept that God has called you to excellence in all things. I'm reminded of this every time I look at a restaurant menu that offers a smorgasbord of different cuisines. Sorry, but there is simply no way a restaurant serving Mexican food and barbecue and pizza and sushi is going to produce any dish with excellence. It's just not possible.* The same is true in our vocations. We can't be anything we want to be and we can't do everything we want to do so long as we are committed to offering the Lord and the world our very best.

> **You can't "do it all" so long as you accept that God has called you to excellence in all things.**

There are two primary limits on our ability to do everything we want to do well: time and attention. Throughout Scripture, God is constantly reminding his people of the brevity of life. We only have so much time on this earth to accomplish the mission God sets before us. For this reason, the biblical authors call for us to carefully consider our lives and to think intentionally about how we are utilizing the time that God has gifted us. Consider James, Jesus's own half brother. In the letter bearing his name, James addressed his readers saying, "What is your life? You are a mist that appears for a little while and then vanishes" (4:14). In John 9:4, Jesus put it this way: "As long as it is day, we must do the works of him who sent me. Night is coming, when no one can work." In light of eternity, we all have but a moment to "do the works of him who sent [us]"—loving God and loving others through excellent work.

But time isn't the only thing limiting our ability to do everything

---

* Unless you're The Cheesecake Factory: the exception that proves the rule.

we want to do with excellence. We also have limited attention. Perhaps one of today's most widely accepted ideas of productivity is that of multitasking, a myth that the scientific community continues to refute in study after study. It turns out that what we refer to as "multitasking" can be more accurately described as "task shifting," with our brains being forced to shift from one task to the other and back again. These shifts in attention don't make us more productive. In fact, they are terribly detrimental to our pursuit of excellence. One study in particular reports that multitasking decreases overall productivity by up to 40 percent![12] In order to do our most excellent work, we must focus our full attention in one direction at a time.

So then, how should we respond to the brutal reality of our limited time and attention? As Christians committed to pursuing excellence in all things and all things for the glory of God, we respond by accepting the fact that we can't do everything we want to do professionally, at least not at the same time. Scattering our time and attention across many disparate endeavors will almost assuredly lead to mediocrity, not mastery. Andrew Carnegie once made this case eloquently to a group of college students, saying:

> The concerns which fail are those which have scattered their
> capital, which means that they have scattered their brains also.
> They have investments in this, or that, or the other, here, there
> and everywhere. "Don't put all your eggs in one basket" is all
> wrong. I tell you "put all your eggs in one basket, and then
> watch that basket." Look round you and take notice; men who
> do that do not often fail. It is easy to watch and carry the one
> basket. It is trying to carry too many baskets that breaks most

eggs in this country. He who carries three baskets must put one
on his head, which is apt to tumble and trip him up. One fault
of the American business man is lack of concentration.[13]

In Ephesians 5:15–16, the apostle Paul implores us to "Be very careful, then, how you live—not as unwise but as wise, making the most of
every opportunity, because the days are evil." In light of the reality of
trade-offs and our limited time and attention, it would be unwise for us
to scatter ourselves across many professional pursuits at the same time.
The wiser path is the one we will be exploring throughout this book,
making every effort to discern the one vocational thing God has called
us to in this season of life and working at it with all our hearts (see Colossians 3:23). It is there—in the pursuit of becoming a master of one—
that we Christians have our best shot of bringing glory to God and
serving our neighbors well through our work. When we say yes to everything, we say yes to nothing, including the unique work the Father
has put us on this earth to do.

Lie #3: Your Happiness Is the Primary Purpose of Work

I've saved the most pervasive and deeply entrenched lie for last, as it re-
ally sets the tone for the rest of this book. For decades, well-intentioned
Christ followers have been doling out a piece of advice that seems loving
on the surface but in reality is quite dangerous. The advice goes some-
thing like this: "Do whatever makes you happy. Follow your passions.
Chase your dreams." Cal Newport, a professor of computer science at
Georgetown University and the best-selling author of *Deep Work* and
So Good They Can't Ignore You, calls this conventional wisdom "the

passion hypothesis" in which we are told that "the key to occupational happiness is to first figure out what you're passionate about and then find a job that matches this passion."[14] As we will see in chapter 5, identifying our God-given passions is an important step on the path to mastery; but making the pursuit of vocational happiness our primary and most immediate aim turns out to be terrible advice.

Why? Put simply, it doesn't work. As scientists are beginning to understand, passion *follows* mastery, not the other way around. In his excellent book *So Good They Can't Ignore You,* Newport cites the work of Amy Wrzesniewski, a professor of organizational behavior at Yale University, who has spent years seeking to understand what leads people across a variety of professions (from doctors to clerical workers and computer programmers) to describe their work as a "calling" as opposed to a "job" or "career." In one study, Wrzesniewski surveyed a group of college administrative assistants, people with the exact same job responsibilities in roles that few people would choose if they were following the overly simplistic advice to just do what you love. In the study, Wrzesniewski discovered that "the strongest predictor of an assistant seeing her work as a calling was the number of years spent on the job. In other words, the more experience an assistant had, the more likely she was to love her work. . . . In Wrzesniewski's research, the happiest, most passionate employees are not those who followed their passion into a position, but instead those who have been around long enough to become good at what they do." Surprisingly, Wrzesniewski was able to find zero evidence to support the conventional wisdom that if you simply seek to do whatever makes you happy by following your passions, you are guaranteed to find a satisfying career. Instead, she discovered that passion is a by-product of mastery.[15]

This startling conclusion flies in the face of conventional wisdom.

In our culture, which demands instant gratification, many of us have bought the lie that we'll discover the deep satisfaction of vocation almost immediately upon finding the job that perfectly matches some preexisting passion. However, that is almost never the case, as scientific studies and the stories of masters throughout this book will show.

As Newport points out, subscribing to the passion hypothesis has dangerous consequences, which, ironically, make us less happy in our work. "The more I studied the issue, the more I noticed that the passion hypothesis convinces people that somewhere there's a magic 'right' job waiting for them, and that if they find it, they'll immediately recognize that this is the work *they were meant to do*," Newport explains. "The problem, of course, is when they fail to find this certainty, bad things follow, such as chronic job-hopping and crippling self-doubt."[16]

As we have already explored, we are seeing more chronic job-hopping today than ever before, with people constantly jumping from gig to gig, intent on finding the immediate satisfaction of vocation, only to be disappointed time and time again. We are failing to take the time to become masterful at any one thing, and this is leading to unprecedented levels of unhappiness. According to Mental Health America, "less than one-third of Americans are happy with their work," and "half of the workforce is 'checked-out.'"[17] We have never had more opportunity to do whatever makes us happy, and yet so few of us love what we do. Clearly, the advice of making our happiness the primary aim of our work isn't working.

> **Following Christ means viewing our entire life (including our work) as service to God and others rather than as a means of getting something from this world.**

For the Christian, this shouldn't come as a surprise. Why? Because this advice is out of line with Jesus's example to serve rather than be served. The passion mind-set focuses exclusively on what value your job offers you. But if our work is to be a calling, we must submit ourselves to the agenda of the One who called us. Following Christ means viewing our entire life (including our work) as service to God and others rather than as a means of getting something from this world.

I don't know if Newport is a Christian, but I do know that he and Wrzesniewski have uncovered a deeply biblical truth at work in the real world: *happiness follows service.* Nowhere in Scripture does it say to follow your passions or do whatever makes you happy. In fact, in some ways, the Bible says the exact opposite. The Christian life is one characterized primarily by service, pouring our lives out as living sacrifices for the sake of God's glory and the good of others (see Romans 12:1). The point of work isn't primarily to make us happy. The point of work is the point of life, summarized by Jesus in Matthew 22: "Love the Lord your God with all your heart and with all your soul and with all your mind. . . . Love your neighbor as yourself" (verses 37, 39).

Let me be clear: I am not saying that our desire to derive happiness from our work is a bad thing. Far from it. In the words of John Piper, "The longing to be happy is a universal human experience, and it is good, not sinful."[18] But, as we will see throughout this book, the way we find the greatest happiness in our work is by prioritizing the joy of God and others above our own, of viewing our work primarily as a means of glorifying God and serving our neighbors rather than ourselves. As we will see in the next two chapters, focused, excellent work accomplishes just that, leading to the deepest, truest, and most sustainable satisfaction of vocation.

Chapter Summary

As Christians we are called to pursue excellence in all things as a means of reflecting the character of our exceptional God. This truth, coupled with the laws of time and trade-offs, means that we simply cannot pursue mastery at many things professionally at the same time. It is precisely because we are called to be excellent in all things that we can't commit to being excellent at many things vocationally.

Key Scripture

"So whether you eat or drink or whatever you do, do it all for the glory of God" (1 Corinthians 10:31).

Next Action*

Which of the three lies of work and calling have you believed most fervently in the past? Take a few minutes to think about this and then summarize in your own words how the scriptures in this chapter helped you replace that lie with biblical truth.

---

* In the "Master of One Notebook," you will find space dedicated to writing out responses to this and other "Next Action" suggestions throughout the book. You can download the free notebook at jordanraynor.com/MOO.

Chapter 2

Proclaiming the Excellencies of God

God is so glorious that it is impossible for you, as his ambassador, to have . . . standards that are too high.

PAUL DAVID TRIPP

The most visited attraction in Barcelona, Spain, is not a theme park, a beach, or a soccer stadium. It's an unfinished church that has been under construction for more than 135 years.[1]

As you approach la Sagrada Família, it's easy to see why more than three million people make the pilgrimage to the church each year. For one thing it is truly awe inspiring, even when compared to Europe's more famous cathedrals such as Notre-Dame in Paris or Westminster Abbey in London. Like something out of a fairy tale, la Sagrada Família resembles the drip sandcastles children make at the beach, only on an extraordinarily larger and more beautiful scale.

As your eyes make their way to the top of this massive structure, the working construction cranes hovering high in the Spanish sky point to the second reason the church is such a draw for world travelers: in an age that prioritizes speed over everything else, the pace at which la Sagrada Família is being built commands our attention. We are used to seeing restaurants get built in weeks, houses go up in months, and skyscrapers rise in just a few years. The idea of spending more than thirteen decades building a single church is simply incomprehensible to most of us. It is that commitment to slow, masterful, excellent work that draws millions of people into this church each year—a church that was intentionally designed to make the world stop and stare at great architecture as a means of pointing us to the glory of God.

Before Antoni Gaudí designed the plans for la Sagrada Família, he had already experienced tremendous success as an architect, using his signature combination of colorful glass and stone to create some of Barcelona's most famous landmarks, including Park Güell and Casa Batlló. But in 1883, at the age of thirty-one, Gaudí began to catch a vision for la Sagrada Família, the project that would become the magnum opus of his career. From the beginning, Gaudí's vision for the church was enormous. A devout Christian, Gaudí envisioned a single church that would visually tell a comprehensive narrative of the life of Christ. "The temple as a whole, as well as being a place for divine worship, will artistically represent the truths of religion and the glorification of God and His Saints," Gaudí said.[2] His vision was a church that would be the physical representation of the Gospels, designed to quite literally "proclaim the excellencies" of God to the world (1 Peter 2:9, ESV).

To do this effectively, Gaudí knew that the church would have to be built on an epic scale. Once construction of the church is completed, la Sagrada Família will be the tallest church building on earth, standing at 560 feet tall. In a conscious effort to prevent his church from surpassing the glory of God's own creation, Gaudí's chosen height for la Sagrada Família is just a few feet short of Montjuïc—the highest natural point in Barcelona. While the height of Gaudí's design is intended to point us to the heavens, it is the rest of this deeply symbolic structure that really declares the glories of God. Once completed, the church will be topped with eighteen spires representing, in ascending order of height, the twelve apostles, the virgin Mary, the four evangelists, and tallest of all, Jesus Christ. At ground level, three grand facades will welcome visitors into the church: the Nativity facade to the east, the Passion facade to the west, and the Glory facade to the south. Today, you can see the completed Nativity and Passion facades, which portray in vivid artistic detail the birth and crucifixion of Jesus Christ. But it's not until visitors step past these facades and into the church that

their jaws really begin to drop. As one well-traveled yet skeptical jour-
nalist said:

> I passed through the door of the nativity façade—and almost at
> once, any doubts were expelled. It is the most astonishing space
> with immediate emotional punch. The scale and colours of the
> interior are truly magnificent. Bone-like columns twist their
> way to the ceiling, branching out from ellipsoid knots, reaching
> upwards, creating the impression of being in an enormous forest.
> Vast geometric stars decorate the ceiling, punctured by open
> hyperboloids, sucking in the light and all suggesting the canopy
> of heaven. The greens, blues, yellows and reds of the light coming
> through [the] stained-glass windows create a dappled effect with
> constantly shifting patterns illuminating the stone, decorated by
> grapes, cherries and flowers. "The heavens declare the glory of
> God; and the firmament sheweth his handywork" is how Psalm
> 19 described creation. Gaudí and his successors just copied it. . . .
> Everywhere you look, the details have been attended to with such
> meticulous care and attention; everything has a meaning in line
> with a desire that the building should be a teaching tool, from
> which the entire history of the church could be read.[3]

Because of Gaudí's commitment to masterful work, la Sagrada
Família quite literally proclaims the gospel to millions of people each
year. What can we learn from Gaudí's example that would inform our
own pursuit of masterful work that glorifies God?

First, Gaudí and his church teach us that excellence requires a tremendous amount of hard work. Gaudi spent forty-three years—more
than half his life—dedicated to la Sagrada Família. No doubt there

were friends and community members urging Gaudí to take shortcuts so he could see some level of completion of his grand vision in his lifetime. But Gaudí would have none of it. Gaudí knew that mastery requires time, and his vision for the church kept him on a slower, more deliberate path. When asked why the church was taking so long to build, Gaudí once commented, "My client is not in a hurry."[4]

There is a second lesson we can draw from Gaudí's story and it is a central theme in this book: masterful work requires tremendous focus. Throughout his four decades working on la Sagrada Família, Gaudí took on fewer and fewer projects until, twelve years prior to his death, he decided to focus exclusively on the building of his church. From 1914 until his death in 1926, Gaudí "dedicated himself exclusively to prayer, to long periods of fasting, and to the construction of la Sagrada Família,"[5] spending most of his days building three-dimensional models of his designs that subsequent generations of architects and craftsmen could follow. A true essentialist, Gaudí went to extremes to eliminate anything from his life that would distract him from his mission of setting la Sagrada Família on a path to its glorious completion after his death. The renowned architect took a vow of poverty, putting himself in the shoes of those his church is meant to serve. In a very real sense, Gaudí poured everything he had into mastering the one thing he believed God was calling him to create. Quite fittingly, Gaudí is buried inside la Sagrada Família, under a headstone that describes the great architect as "a man of exemplary life, and an extraordinary craftsman, the author of this marvelous work."[6]

Today, dozens of craftspeople continue the work Gaudí started, working diligently to bring la Sagrada Família to its highly anticipated completion (currently slated for 2026). But with an annual construction budget of nearly $30 million, this work continues amidst significant debate and controversy, with some arguing that those funds would be better spent more directly on the poor the building is meant to serve. But there's no denying that this costly masterpiece-in-the-making has already produced something of great and increasingly rare value. In an age in which we are addicted to rapid production, quick fixes, fast food, and speed at the cost of everything else, the sheer excellence of la Sagrada Família commands our attention. Then, once it grabs us, the magnificent architecture redirects our gaze to the glory of God and the life of his Son, causing us to yearn to learn more about the exceptional character of the God the church seeks to reflect.

While most of our work will not proclaim the excellencies of God quite as literally as Gaudí's la Sagrada Família, all of us are commanded to do whatever we do "all for the glory of God" (1 Corinthians 10:31). That means that whether you're a doctor, a sales rep, a janitor, an architect, an athlete, a stay-at-home mom, or an entrepreneur, one of the primary purposes of your work is to glorify God. How do we bring God glory? We reflect his greatness and character to the world. As we've seen, one of his most obvious characteristics is that of excellence. You can't stare out at the Grand Canyon and not marvel at the masterful work of God. You can't go to a zoo without appreciating the creative supremacy of the Creator. And you can't hold a baby without wondering at the excellence it takes to make millions of cells form together to create life. We worship the preeminent God. A perfect God. *Excellent* is far too trite a word to describe the God of the universe, but it is the closest we mere mortals can come to understand. Theologian Andreas J. Köstenberger wrote:

God is the grounds of all true excellence. He is the one who fills
any definition of excellence with meaning, and he is the reason
why we cannot be content with lackluster mediocrity, half-
hearted effort, or substandard [work]. Excellence starts and ends
with God and is first and foremost a hallmark and attribute of
God. Without God as our starting point and continual frame
of reference, our discussion of excellence would be hopelessly
inadequate.[7]

How then are we to respond to the excellent character of our heavenly Father? In short, we respond by imitating his excellence in everything we do, including our work. I love how novelist-turned-apologist
Dorothy Sayers put it in her classic essay, "Why Work?"

> [Work] should be looked upon, not as a necessary drudgery
> to be undergone for the purpose of making money, but as a
> way of life in which the nature of man should find its proper
> exercise and delight and so fulfill itself to the glory of God.
> That it should, in fact, be thought of as a creative activity
> undertaken for the love of the work itself; and that man, made
> in God's image, should make things, as God makes them, for
> the sake of doing well a thing that is well worth doing. . . .

> The Church's approach to an intelligent carpenter is usually
> confined to exhorting him not to be drunk and disorderly in
> his leisure hours, and to come to church on Sundays. What the
> Church should be telling him is this: that the very first demand
> that his religion makes upon him is that he should make good
> tables. . . .

[The Church] has forgotten that the secular vocation is sacred. Forgotten that a building must be good architecture before it can be a good church; that a painting must be well painted before it can be a good sacred picture; that work must be good work before it can call itself God's work.[8]

In other words, we glorify God when we imitate his character of excellence and in doing so "proclaim the excellencies of him who called you out of darkness into his marvelous light" (1 Peter 2:9, ESV). We live surrounded by darkness in a world that is desperate for something excellent and true. There is perhaps no more influential sphere of life for us to shine the light of Christ than in our chosen work. When we work with excellence, we have the great privilege of being able to glorify God and proclaim his excellencies to the world around us.

In Ephesians 5:1, Paul likened our efforts to glorify God to the way children naturally imitate their parents when he commanded, "Therefore be imitators of God, as beloved children" (ESV). I love this verse because I think we can all understand how the actions of children reflect (for better or worse) the character of their parents. My wife, Kara, and I volunteer in the nursery at our church, and every so often we have one of "those kids" in our class—a toddler who spends the full ninety minutes pushing over towering toys, stealing snacks, and deliberately disobeying authority. One Sunday morning, after the umpteenth time correcting a child like this, I looked at my wife and asked, "Who are this kid's

> **When we work with excellence, we have the great privilege of being able to glorify God and proclaim his excellencies to the world around us.**

parents?" In more subtle ways, the world is asking the same question of you and me. If we say our Father is so good, loving, and excellent, our actions as his children ought to reflect his character. We are the physical representations of God in this world, which is precisely why God has called us to work with excellence, doing everything for his glory. Again, the theologian Köstenberger is worth quoting at some length:

> As God's redeemed children, we are to strive to be like God. This, it appears, includes striving for excellence. . . .
>
> Our creation in God's image, therefore, primarily relates to the fact that God placed humanity on the earth to rule it as his representatives. How can we best fulfill this role? It stands to reason that as beings created in God's image, creatures who are called to exercise representative rule over his creation, we must do so with excellence. . . . The world desperately needs to see a display of what God is like. This extends to everything we are and do—our own personal lives, our marriages and families, our moral and ethical standards, and the pursuit of our calling. . . .
>
> Since excellence, then, is an all-encompassing attribute of God, and since we are exhorted in Scripture to imitate God, having been made in his likeness, excellence should mark our lives as his children, extending both to who we are (our character and our relationships) and what we do (our work or vocation). . . .
>
> Excellence is in fact a divine mandate that applies to every aspect of our lives, for God himself is characterized by excellence. Mediocrity, sloppy workmanship, and a half-hearted effort do not bring glory to God or advance his kingdom.[9]

Slamming his fist against the bathroom stall, David Boudia broke down sobbing. This was not how he envisioned his Olympics ending. Boudia, a diver for the US team, had come to Beijing in 2008 determined to bring home a gold medal. Instead, he finished tenth in his event, seemingly miles away from the coveted Olympic podium.

Shortly after Boudia's disappointing performance, USA Diving hosted a party for the entire team at a restaurant in Beijing. "I suffered through it as one of the worst experiences of my life," Boudia recalled. "The whole party was a somber occasion. I think everyone was bummed because, once again, we didn't win any medals in diving. But the sorrow may have been more painful for me. It was my fault we didn't win any medals. I was in the last event. I could have delivered. . . . Mentally drained, I couldn't put on a tough-guy face anymore. I still didn't let anyone see me cry, but I left the dinner party and locked myself in a bathroom stall, where all the heartache and disappointment came pouring out in a torrent of tears."[10]

Nobody makes it to the Olympics without passionately pursuing mastery of their sport. Olympians are "the best of the best of the best,"* but they don't get there by accident. Elite athletes know that excellence requires years of purposeful practice and discipline (subjects we will explore further in chapter 8). But as Boudia's story so powerfully demonstrates, there's a world of difference between being motivated to pursue excellence for your own glory and pursuing excellence for the glory of God.

Like so many world-class athletes, Boudia was laser focused on the Olympics from an early age. After being mesmerized by the 1996

---

* A reference for my fellow *Men in Black* fans. "With honors!"

Olympics at the age of seven, "competing in the Olympics became my focus, my inspiration, my dream, my god," Boudia explained. "I was going to be an Olympian. Not only that, but I was going to win—and I would revel in the fame and the celebrity it brought. And in the years that followed, I bowed at the feet of gods fashioned of gold, silver, and bronze."[11]

For Boudia, dreams of Olympic medals represented the more deeply entrenched idols in his heart. Like so many others, he wasn't motivated to pursue excellence for the sheer joy of mastering a craft and revealing the character of God in the process. "My only desire in life was to please myself," Boudia noted. "A gold medal would mean fame and adoration. A gold medal would mean success. It would mean acceptance. It would mean happiness and joy. So, relentlessly and doggedly, that's what I chased."[12]

It was clear from a young age that Boudia had a real shot at Olympic glory, either in gymnastics (his first sport) or in diving. For years his athletic success delivered the emotional high Boudia was looking for, feeding his desire for recognition and acceptance. But it didn't take long for Boudia to recognize that these were counterfeit gods. "When you live for the praise of other people, you can never be satisfied," he said, reflecting on his early years as a competitive athlete. "The ecstasy from a win today quickly fades, and you have to win tomorrow to recapture that high. It's a relentless, unsatisfying, and elusive quest when you are fueled by the pursuit of your own glory."[13]

That "elusive quest" is what led Boudia to angrily rage against the bathroom stall in Beijing. While his teammates, coaches, and parents were enjoying just being at the Olympics, Boudia couldn't handle the agony of defeat. "My god had betrayed me," Boudia said. "The one I had served for so long, the one I had worked for and sacrificed for, the one whose approval I so desperately sought, the one I was willing to do anything to appease had toyed with me and promised me something that it didn't deliver. It had beaten me down and crushed me in return for all I had given. Never in my life had I been so distraught."[14]

After leaving Beijing, Boudia returned to school at Purdue University and entered the deepest depression of his life. One night, while the rest of campus watched the Purdue Boilermakers take on Notre Dame on the football field, Boudia locked himself in his dorm room and seriously considered taking his own life. "Nothing made sense to me whatsoever, and I felt emptier than I had my entire life," Boudia shared. "I sat there looking at an orange wall in my room, thinking that life was pointless. I was desperate for relief from my hopeless existence. I thought this life was pointless, and I wanted it to be over. What I didn't know was that life was just about to begin."[15]

Boudia pulled out his phone and texted Ashley Karnes, a diving teammate he used to party with who had recently started opting out of that lifestyle. Karnes suggested that Boudia text their coach, Adam Soldati, a Christian who had earned the respect of Boudia, Karnes, and other divers. Willing to try anything to relieve his deep emotional pain, Boudia texted Soldati, who suggested they get together the next day.

When Boudia arrived at Soldati's home, he wasn't sure what to expect. He surely wasn't expecting to be presented with the gospel. But that's precisely what Soldati did. As Boudia recalled, "Adam gently pointed out that given my struggles, the way I had been living didn't seem to be working out too well. He was absolutely right. Living for myself and my own pleasures had gotten me nowhere fast. . . . God had given me that hunger and thirst for satisfaction that could only be found in a relationship with him."[16]

That conversation changed Boudia's life forever, bringing him to saving faith in Jesus Christ and radically changing how he viewed his work as a diver. Boudia understood that because God loved him, he no longer had to earn gold medals to win God's favor. He was loved and accepted just as he was.

At first this led Boudia to lose his appetite and passion for diving and nearly abandon his one professional thing. But through the wise counsel of his pastor, Boudia came to realize that he could continue to pursue mastery of his craft as a diver not for his own glory but with the redeemed ambition that seeks to reveal the greatness of God through excellent work. "In those sessions with [my pastor], he began teaching me that just because I was a Christian, and just because Jesus was my highest priority, that didn't give me license to slack off in the other areas of my life. That wasn't glorifying to God," Boudia said. "[He] showed me that God had given me my ability to dive, and that was a platform for me to share the testimony of what God had done for me. I didn't understand it at the time, but I slowly began to learn that I could dive for a purpose. That purpose was to be a visible representation of an invisible God."[17]

Boudia was coming to learn the truth we have been exploring in this chapter: the purpose of focused, masterful work isn't for our own glory but to glorify God by reflecting his character of excellence to the world. It was only after Boudia found this redeemed purpose for his work as a diver that he regained his ambition for the sport. "Once those lessons took root in my life, I started to pour my heart into diving practice again," Boudia explained. "I began working hard and not neglecting my responsibilities. It's easy for me to push my duties aside if I don't want to do them, but my growth in the Lord showed me that a man after God's heart does hard things."[18]

With ambition rooted in a desire to proclaim the excellencies of

God rather than making a name for himself, Boudia worked harder and with more focus than ever before. Once again, he was focused on winning the Olympic games. "But this time," Boudia said, "I would not zealously chase a gold medal and worldly success to satisfy my selfish desires for glory. This time, I would be solely concerned with bringing glory to God. . . . This time, I would do my best and be content with whatever the results were, as long as I was doing everything to please the Lord by being a witness for him."[19]

Since Boudia's radical conversion he has experienced both victory and defeat in the pool. At the 2012 Olympics in London, Boudia fulfilled his lifelong dream of standing on the podium with a gold medal around his neck. However, in 2016, Boudia and his partner, Steele Johnson, finished second to the Chinese in the synchronized diving event at the Olympics in Rio de Janeiro. But instead of spending the night punching a bathroom stall, Boudia had deep, genuine joy. In a postdive interview, a reporter asked the duo how they were holding up after finishing second in an event with "a whole lot of pressure." Boudia replied, "When my mind is on [diving] and thinking I'm defined by [diving], then my mind goes crazy. But we both know that our identity is in Christ." Johnson (also a Christian) added, "The fact that I was going into this event knowing that my identity is rooted in Christ and not what the result of this competition is gave me peace, gave me ease, and it let me enjoy the contest."[20]

> **Because the gospel frees us from the *requirement* to win, we gain a deep *desire* to master our work and proclaim the excellencies of God in the process.**

The divers' comments reflect an important point that is critical for us to understand: in victory or defeat, success or failure, we can glorify God by passionately pursuing excellence and seeking to be the very best version of who God created us to be. Nowhere in Scripture does God command success or certain levels of performance. Because of the work of Jesus on our behalf, we don't need to use our work in some misguided attempt to save ourselves or, like a younger Boudia, to prove to the world that we are valuable. We are valuable and worthy because Christ loves us, not because of any level of success we may attain in our careers. It is that very security in Christ alone that frees us to pursue mastery in our work for his glory rather than our own. And *that* is what leads us to "work heartily, as for the Lord and not for men" (Colossians 3:23, esv), giving us the deep, lasting, sustainable ambition to work with the highest standards of excellence. Because the gospel frees us from the *requirement* to win, we gain a deep *desire* to master our work and proclaim the excellencies of God in the process.

As Boudia shared, "Christians follow the Lord by doing everything with excellence because God does all things with excellence. Being excellent is a character trait of God, so when we pursue it, we are modeling ourselves after him. When I compete, I'm doing it for the glory of God. In any given competition I can be a finger pointing to God's goodness and a light shining on his faithfulness. I don't have to tear others down or do whatever it takes to win. If I choose to do it that way, that's disobedience and a perversion of what God requires of us. But to work hard and do my best, to love others around me, that brings honor to God when I'm on the platform."[21]

As exemplified by Boudia and Gaudí, one of the purposes of focused, masterful work is demonstrating our love for our Father by reflecting his image and character of excellence to the world around us.

We'll see in the next chapter that exceptional work also helps us follow the second Greatest Commandment: loving our neighbors as ourselves.

Chapter Summary

As God's children we are called to be his image bearers, reflecting his character of excellence in every aspect of life, including our work. Thus, one of the most fundamental purposes of pursuing mastery in our work is the pursuit of God's glory. We glorify him and proclaim his excellencies when we do our work masterfully well.

Key Scripture

"But you are a chosen race, a royal priesthood, a holy nation, a people for his own possession, that you may proclaim the excellencies of him who called you out of darkness into his marvelous light" (1 Peter 2:9, ESV).

Next Action

Write a prayer praising God for his character of excellence and asking him to guide you as you pursue mastery in your work for his glory.

Chapter 3

The Ministry of Excellence

If you are a craftsman you will find the Bible placed in your workshop, in your hands, in your heart; it teaches and preaches how you ought to treat your neighbor. Only look at your tools, your needle, your thimble, your beer barrel, your articles of trade, your scales, your measures, and you will find this saying written on them . . . "use me toward your neighbor as you would want him to act toward you with that which is his."

MARTIN LUTHER

Jessica Jones has always passionately pursued excellence in her work as a nurse practitioner in the neonatal intensive care unit (NICU). Her career started with an internship at the prestigious Children's Hospital of Philadelphia where she learned from some of the best doctors in the world how to care for sick and premature newborn babies. Since then, Jones has treated hundreds of babies, consoled as many mothers and fathers, and acquired thousands of hours of purposeful practice, spending years getting masterful at her one vocation.

While Jones has always had high standards of excellence in her work, it was when she became a mother herself that her motivation for mastery at her craft reached a new and higher level. "Becoming a mom changed everything for me," Jones said. "My first few weeks back to work after the birth of my first child were difficult. Every sick baby I saw could have been my baby. I think there's a certain compassion and understanding that women gain when they enter motherhood. Working in the NICU and seeing these moms in their most vulnerable state tends to magnify that. Before I was a mom, I think I had a pretty good idea of what it looked like to 'love my neighbor' through my work. But after the birth of my son, I had a much greater appreciation for what it meant to 'love my neighbor *as myself*' and that motivated me to get even better at my job."

Even today, with nearly two decades of experience to her credit, Jones is continuing to push herself to be an even better medical professional, asking doctors for feedback on her work, spending her downtime in the hospital reading medical journals, and regularly praying that God would continue to develop her skills as a nurse practitioner. What drives Jones in this persistent pursuit of excellence? "I truly see my work as ministry," she said.

When you first hear Jones describe her work as "ministry," you might assume that she spends hours praying or sharing the gospel with her patients' parents, who are often searching for hope when their newborn baby is in such a fragile state. "While there have certainly been situations in which I've had the opportunity to minister to patients in that way, it is far from the norm. That's not primarily what I mean when I describe my work as ministry," Jones explained. "I have the unique opportunity to be around families at the most exciting and often the scariest time of their lives. I have a chance to not just be good at what I do, but to do my work with excellence because I am doing it for a higher purpose, and that is to show the love of Christ to my neighbor, to those mothers and fathers who are hurting and scared."

Jones understands that while excellent work often produces influence, power, and opportunities for Christians to share the gospel, those good things are not the primary purpose of mastery. The most fundamental reason why we Christians ought to pursue excellence in our work is to bring glory to God and love our neighbors as ourselves. "I am doing ministry when I do my work with excellence," Jones shared, "taking my God-given gifts and using them to the best of my ability to bring these newborns back to full health. That is how I love my neighbor as myself."[1]

> **As Christians, we can't say we are seeking to love our neighbor as ourselves and then do our work with mediocrity.**

In many ways Jones is everything you would want in a medical professional who is treating your child. She is kind, warm, and patient, but most important to her patients, Jones is masterful at her craft. Most parents of Jones's patients aren't interested to know if she goes to church, what her religious beliefs are, or if she wears a cross around her neck. At the end of the day, they don't really care if she is warm and personable. When their children's lives are on the line, all these parents care about is whether or not Jones is a master of her craft and whether or not she is able to bring their babies back to full health. The primary purpose of Jones's excellent work is loving and serving her neighbors as she would want another medical professional to serve her child if she were on the other side of the waiting room.

As we will see in part 3 of this book, the promise of masterful work is great: God uses our excellent work to make Christians winsome to the world, leading to opportunities to share the gospel and do what many would consider more overt ministry. While all these gifts are wonderful, God-honoring things that should motivate us in our pursuit of mastery, they are not the most fundamental purpose of excellent work, as Jones's testimony makes clear. We ought to pursue excellence in our work not as a means to an end, but as a simple act of obedience to the Lord's command to glorify God and, in the words of Jesus, to "love your neighbor as yourself" (Matthew 22:39).

Notice that, in summarizing the Greatest Commandments, Jesus didn't say, "Love your neighbor as yourself . . . so that you can share the gospel," or "Love your neighbor as yourself . . . in order to obtain cultural influence." "Love your neighbor as yourself" was a complete sentence. Simply loving our neighbor is good and God-honoring in and of itself and is the foundational purpose for focused, masterful work, as well as the most fundamental way we make ourselves useful to the world. As Christians, we can't say we are seeking to love our neighbor as ourselves and then do our work with mediocrity. In some professions (like Jones's), mediocre work can result in the loss of life. For most of us the relative skill of our work isn't going to mean the difference between life and death, but we all have an opportunity to obey Jesus's command to love our neighbors as ourselves by choosing to do excellent work. My friend Matt Perman provides a great example of this in his book *What's Best Next*:

> One summer after some especially heavy rains, three sump pumps went out on our street, all on the same day. . . . The reason, as we eventually learned, is that the builders decided to use the cheapest sump pumps they could find rather than spending a couple hundred dollars more to get higher quality pumps. The result of their poor workmanship was a flooded basement.
>
> The builder was seeking to save himself a few hundred dollars on each house built, but in order to do so, he passed a far greater cost onto me, the owner. I paid with my time and an insurance deductible, and my insurance company paid for new carpet and baseboards. Our builder made life easier on himself at the cost of making it harder on us.
>
> That is not what I would call good work . . . .
>
> Christians are to . . . do work that will truly benefit people by going the extra mile rather than just doing the minimum necessary. Excellence in our work is actually a form of generosity and *love,* and poor quality is a form of stinginess and selfish-

ness. Shoddy work is not just shoddy work; it's a failure of love.

This means we are to be generous not just with the results of our work but also *in* our work. One of the best forms of generosity in our work is *excellence*. Excellence matters not only because it is right and exciting in itself, but even more significantly because it is a way of serving people.[2]

Expounding upon this same idea, pastor Timothy Keller said, "One of the main ways that you love others in your work is through the 'ministry of competence.' If God's purpose for your job is that you serve the human community, then the way to serve God best is to do the job as well as it can be done."[3]

Keller is spot-on; but I think it's necessary to extend Keller's comments beyond the idea of "competence," as that word often connotes simple adequacy or a baseline standard that one must achieve in order to call a job done. We might say that the builder of Perman's home was competent as he technically got the job done and delivered a home that was inhabitable by Perman and his family. But nobody would say this builder did his work masterfully well, and that unwillingness to go the extra mile produced suffering for his neighbor—the very opposite of love. As Christians we are called to much more than mere competency in our chosen work. We are called to mastery, striving for excellence in all things, and it is through the ministry of *excellence* that we best love our neighbors through our work.

> **It is through the ministry of excellence that we best love our neighbors through our work.**

If the church were to embrace this generous, selfless, sacrificial vision for excellent work, the world would have to take notice, as this approach to work is so countercultural today. Perhaps no book summarizes the metanarrative of our culture's view on work better than *The 4-Hour Workweek* by Tim Ferriss. I have long had a complicated relationship with this book. I love *The 4-Hour Workweek* because I think Ferriss offers some brilliant, practical tips for how to be more productive in life, but I strongly disagree with the reasons why so many people are subscribing to Ferriss's helpful life hacks. Most of the Ferriss disciples I've met through the years are desperately trying to figure out how they can do the bare minimum amount of work needed to support a luxury lifestyle, jet-set around the world, and spend their days kicking back on a hammock on the beach.

This is not the picture the Bible paints for the life of the Christian. Yes, the Bible is clear that we should enjoy the good gifts God has given us in this life. But as the life of Christ so beautifully demonstrates, we aren't here on this earth primarily to maximize our pleasure. Our purpose isn't *to use* the world but to be of the utmost *use to* the world. Our purpose is to glorify God and love others, thereby reflecting the life of Christ. In the words of Paul in Romans 12:1, "In view of God's mercy," we are called to "offer [our] bodies as a living sacrifice," going far beyond the minimum standards in our chosen work and passionately pursuing excellence for the glory of God and the good of others. I love how John Mark Comer puts it:

> God made the world, not to get something from us, but rather
> as a gift for us to enjoy and play in and make something of. In
> the same way, when we live and work, not to get what we can
> from others, but rather to love and serve them, we're harmo-

nizing with the heart of God himself. And one of the best possible ways we can love and serve people is to show up for work every day. And to do our work, not to get ahead, or make more money, or become famous, but to love and serve God and neighbor. And when we do that, we start to reclaim our humanness.[4]

As Comer put so well, the purpose of mastery isn't to acquire our own fame or fortune. The purpose of mastery is to glorify God and love our neighbors as ourselves. As Christians we shouldn't seek to do the bare minimum in our jobs to collect a paycheck. If we believe our work is a calling from God, we will "work heartily, as for the Lord," seeking to glorify God and love others well by being the very best nurse practitioners, entrepreneurs, teachers, artists, carpenters, and executives we can possibly be. Our desire to love our neighbors through the ministry of excellence will lead us to view our work more sacrificially; and as the following story of Cynthia Marshall shows, it will also cause us to work with a tremendous amount of focus.

When Mark Cuban placed the phone call, he was hoping to reach Cynthia Marshall. Instead, Marshall's husband, Kenneth, picked up the line since his wife was on another call. Assuming a call from a celebrity like Cuban was a good enough reason to interrupt his wife, Kenneth caught Cynthia's attention, motioned to the phone, and loudly whispered, "It's Mark Cuban!"

"Who?" Cynthia whispered back.

"Shark Tank!" Kenneth replied.

Cynthia responded with a blank stare.

"The *billionaire* . . . the owner of the Dallas Mavericks," Kenneth continued, looking for a reaction from his wife. Still nothing. Now realizing that his wife had never heard of Cuban before, Kenneth insisted: "Get off that phone!"[5]

Mark Cuban was in crisis mode, and he was calling to ask for Cynthia's help. The #MeToo movement was in full swing, with women all around the world bravely coming forward to name high-profile men who had sexually harassed them. The wave of scandals had already taken down titans of entertainment, politics, and sports, but a new investigative report by *Sports Illustrated* had exposed the Dallas Mavericks organization and its former CEO Terdema Ussery, as one of the most egregious cases reported to date. The article cited more than a dozen former Mavericks employees who told abhorrent stories of verbal and sexual harassment over the course of two decades, painting a picture of "a corporate culture rife with misogyny and predatory sexual behavior." One former Mavericks employee described the organization as "a real life *Animal House*."[6]

Recognizing the magnitude of the problem on his hands, Cuban moved quickly to fix the Mavericks' culture. While he had already kicked off an independent investigation into the allegations, he knew that wasn't enough. Cuban needed a new CEO to radically transform the Mavericks' toxic environment. Through his search he learned about Cynthia Marshall, who seemed like the perfect fit. Marshall was recommended to Cuban by executives at AT&T, where Marshall had spent thirty-six years as a highly respected human resources executive. Marshall's former colleagues assured Cuban that she was the perfect person to turn around the Mavericks organization. If she accepted Cuban's offer, Marshall would become the first female African American CEO in the NBA's seventy-two-year history.

The fact that Marshall was being offered this position is an incredible testament to God's sovereignty and grace. Marshall grew up in the projects outside San Francisco. While the hardship of economic poverty was certainly tough on Marshall, her siblings, and her mother, it was nothing compared to the emotional and physical pain inflicted on the family by Marshall's father. On one occasion Marshall stepped between her mother and her father's fist, taking a blow to the face, which broke her nose.[7] When she was fifteen, Marshall's father left the family, but not before delivering some final verbal abuse. As Marshall recalled, "He told me and my youngest sister that we would be hookers on the street without him. I told my sister, 'That's not true. We are going to be the first in this family to graduate from college. I'm going to get mom out of these projects.'"[8]

All of this trauma at such a formative age had a huge impact on Marshall's vision for her future. Given her upbringing, Marshall decided quickly what she wanted to do with her career: she would excel in the discipline of human resources. Knowing firsthand the tremendous pain verbal and physical abuse can inflict, Marshall wanted to spend her career loving others well, and she knew it was going to take a tremendous amount of sacrifice and focus to do that work with excellence.

Just a few years after her father abandoned her family, Marshall made good on her promise, becoming the first in her family to go to college. She received a full scholarship to the University of California, Berkeley, where she earned two degrees: one in human resources management and another in business administration.[9] Throughout college, Marshall's desire to love her neighbor as herself pushed her to pursue her work with great intensity. She remembers thinking, "I have too many people depending on me and these people told me to focus. I said, 'I gotta focus.'" In fact, she was so focused that she broke up with her boyfriend during her first week of college so that she could concentrate on her schoolwork. Marshall told her boyfriend, "I'll call you when I graduate," she recalled. "I told him I have to focus. I told him I don't have time for some smooth-talking cutie who wants to play when I need to study." On graduation day Marshall did call her ex-boyfriend, Kenneth, to whom she has been married for nearly thirty years.[10]

Marshall's intense focus on mastering her one thing paid off. Almost immediately after graduating from Berkeley, Marshall landed a job at AT&T, where she quickly moved up the corporate ladder and became known as an excellent and compassionate human resources executive. By the time she retired from AT&T thirty-six years later, she had risen to the position of chief diversity officer and senior vice president of human resources, a role that made her responsible for developing and directing human resources programs for AT&T's 240,000 employees. Marshall spent more than three decades mastering the practice of human resources, putting herself in a position to serve nearly a quarter of a million people, working to ensure that all of AT&T's employees were emotionally and physically safe—a luxury Marshall wishes she had as a young woman.

By the time Mark Cuban called, Marshall had retired from AT&T and was looking forward to the next chapter of her career as a consultant. But Cuban was hoping to convince Marshall to step back into full-time service, this time leveraging her masterful skills as a human resources executive to serve other women in what was now one of the most closely watched organizations in the world. As her husband quickly realized, Marshall had no clue who Cuban was. Furthermore, she knew nothing about the *Sports Illustrated* exposé on Cuban's Mavericks. After agreeing to meet with the team's billionaire owner, she picked up a copy of the magazine. "And I'm reading about it, and I'm getting sick," Marshall recalled. "Like, what's going on in this place? I mean, this culture's bad. I don't know if I want to do this."[11]

In fact, Marshall was pretty certain she didn't want the job as CEO of the Mavericks. But after meeting some of the women within the Mavericks organization, she knew she had to accept Cuban's offer. As she looked into their eyes and shook their hands, these women said, "We need you. We absolutely need you."[12] Like the rest of the world, Marshall was sick of the seemingly endless barrage of sexual harassment allegations. As Marshall recalled, "I'm yelling at the TV all the time when something happens, when the #MeToo stuff is coming out, saying this is ridiculous. How can that happen?"[13] Due to her focused commitment to her one thing, Marshall had the skills and expertise to fix the Mavericks' problems and love her neighbors as herself in the process. "When [Cuban's] call came, I thought, I can't just sit on the sidelines. Instead of yelling at the TV, I'm being called into service. I'm doing this for the sisterhood."[14]

An interviewer once asked Marshall what she wants people to think about when they remember her. Her response was simple: "That she loves God and she loves people."[15] Through focused, excellent work, Marshall does exactly that. By pursuing mastery of her one thing, the Lord has used Marshall to love and serve the vulnerable she feels called to protect.

———

As we have seen in the first part of this book, the purpose of mastery in our work is not to accumulate fame and fortune for ourselves or to subsidize our lifestyle. It's not even primarily a means to earn credibility and power or to share the gospel. The most fundamental purpose of mastery is the same as our purpose in life: to glorify God and love and serve others as ourselves. As the masters in these chapters have demonstrated, focused, excellent work accomplishes just that. Antoni Gaudí showed us how a commitment to masterful work produced a church that declares the glory of God nearly a hundred years after the great architect's death. David Boudia demonstrates what it looks like practically to be motivated to pursue mastery for the glory of God rather than personal gain. And Jessica Jones and Cynthia Marshall show us how focused, masterful work allows us to live out the ministry of excellence, loving our neighbors as ourselves.

The case I have been building up to this point is that as Christians we live out the Greatest Commandments through our vocations when we do our work with focus and excellence. With this as our foundation, there are still a number of big questions for us to answer. For starters, what are the practical ways we can discern which work God has equipped us to do masterfully well? How do we know when we've found the one thing the Lord is calling us to do? Once we have a clear path, how do we eliminate things that are distracting us from our chosen work? Finally, what can we learn from scientific research and the stories of Christ-following masters about how to become masterful in our one thing? Those are the questions we now turn to in part 2.

Chapter Summary

If the first, most fundamental purpose of masterful work is to bring God glory, the second is to love our neighbors as ourselves. We ought to pursue excellence in our work not as a means to an end but in obedience to what Jesus identified as the Greatest Commandments. As Christians we can't claim to love our neighbor as ourselves and then do our work with mediocrity. Mediocre work is nothing short of a failure of love. It is through the ministry of excellence that we love our neighbors through our work.

Key Scripture

"Love the Lord your God with all your heart and with all your soul and with all your mind. . . . Love your neighbor as yourself" (Matthew 22:37–39).

Next Action

Write down one thing you could do in your current work to go beyond the minimum standards and more excellently serve your employer, employees, or customers.

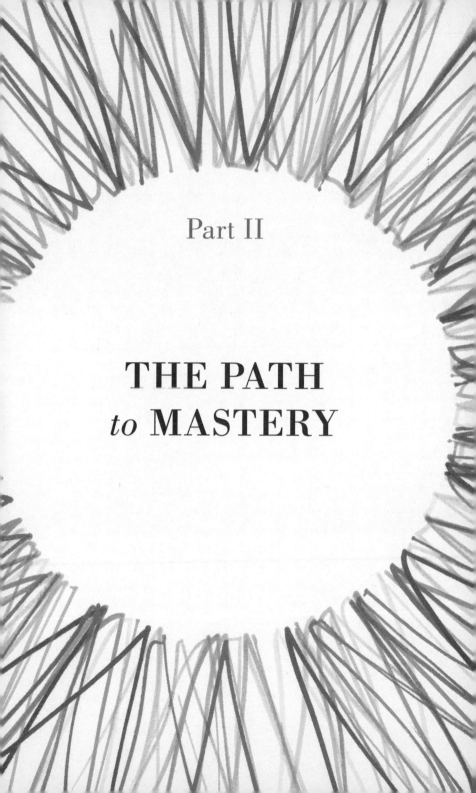

Part II

THE PATH
to MASTERY

Chapter 4

Start with "The One" in Mind

Do one thing. And do one thing well. And
do that one thing well as an act of service and
love for the world and to the glory of God.

JOHN MARK COMER

Hollywood's portrayal of the quest for romantic love is so consistent it has become cliché. Movie after movie tell the story of a guy or girl on a mystical journey to find the one person he or she is destined to be with for the rest of their lives. And this search isn't characterized by choice. Rather, it is a quest driven by destiny to find one perfect person out of the more than seven billion people on planet Earth.

I think most of us have come to realize that this narrative of love is illogical and untrue. The reality is that there are likely hundreds of people in this world who share our values, faith, and dreams and would make great partners for us in marriage. However, while we accept these facts, many of us still embrace a similar romanticized view of finding the one thing God has called us to do professionally. The truth is, just as we each have many potential lifetime partners, there are many things you and I could do masterfully well in our vocations in order to bring God great glory and serve others well. As we have already seen, God certainly gives us unique passions and gifts that make us more likely to excel in one vocation over another, but in his grace, God has given us the ability to *choose* our work. There is not just one Mr. Right for our careers, but there is a Mr. Best. In this second part of the book, we will examine how to explore our vocational options to make the best possible choice of our one thing, and then, once we've chosen a path, how precisely we can become masterful at our chosen work.

Before we begin that journey together, we need to be crystal clear about what we are looking for in our one thing. It would be a waste of time and energy to explore various vocations with no precise idea of what it is we're looking for at the end of the road. Before we can start down this path, we need to know exactly where we are heading. We need to start with "the one" in mind.

Broad or Specific

At the start of this path to finding, focusing on, and mastering your one vocational thing, it's important to understand that your one thing might be very specific or quite broad.

For example, my friend Bob Horton's one thing is *crazy* specific: Bob tunes pianos. That's it. That's all he does and that's all that he's been doing professionally for more than three decades. Not surprisingly, he is an absolute master of his craft. Maybe God has called you, like Bob, to master something super specific. Or perhaps your one thing is much broader. Take C. S. Lewis as an example. Lewis is best known for authoring classic books such as *The Chronicles of Narnia, Mere Christianity,* and *The Screwtape Letters.* This may lead you to believe that Lewis's one thing was writing, but when I sat down to chat with his stepson Douglas Gresham, it became clear that Lewis's one thing was much broader. "I'm not entirely sure that mastery as a writer was his primary thing," Gresham told me. "He really was an amazing teacher and one who became immensely popular through his writings because of his considerable teaching abilities. So that came first. I think writing was a second string to his bow as it were. The writing was a means to that end. I think his one thing was teaching. He was a teacher in practically everything he did."[1]

And Lewis did a lot. In addition to his work as an author, Lewis applied his masterful teaching skills in a variety of other roles, including as a teacher of English language and literature at Oxford's Magdalen College and a radio broadcaster for the BBC, helping the British people process big questions about God, humanity, and life during World War II. At first glance these roles may look disconnected, and thus Lewis may have appeared to be unfocused in his career. But the common thread throughout Lewis's writing, lecturing, and broadcasting was his one vocational thing: teaching. Lewis recognized that God had given him unique abilities as a teacher, and he worked with an incredible amount of discipline to hone that single craft and apply it in many different contexts.

My own story began more like Bob's, but (thus far) has ended up looking more like Lewis's. In the eighth grade I was certain I knew what my one thing was: I was going to run political campaigns. Yes, I was "that kid," and I remained focused on my very specific one thing throughout high school. Just before graduation I accepted an offer to run a countywide campaign in my hometown of Tampa, Florida. After the candidate won that campaign, I was hooked, more confident than ever that running campaigns was going to be the one thing I committed to mastering in my career.

However, almost immediately after I started courses at Florida State University, my interests began to broaden significantly, taking my career in a bunch of different directions as I explored which work I could do best. Something as narrow and specific as running political campaigns could no longer hold my attention and ambition. By the time I was a few years out of college (and was having lunch with my mentor Rick, whom you'll recall from the introduction), I no longer had clarity on the work I was going to "sink my teeth into" and pursue mastery of professionally. I was making a millimeter of progress in a million different directions. Over time, and with much prayer and exploration (a subject we'll learn more about in the next chapter), I came to see that the one thing God had equipped and called me to do most exceptionally well professionally was the work of an entrepreneur. I realized I was gifted at the art of understanding people's problems, bringing products to market to solve those problems, and setting up systems for those products to thrive over time. I leveraged those skills specifically for political campaigns, but I realized I could also apply them to my other interests.

Entrepreneurship is the one thing I have chosen to go big on and master at this stage of my career; and while my one thing is fairly broad (much like teaching was for Lewis), it is applied with laser-like focus to just one or two projects at a time. As I mentioned in the introduction, when I started writing this book, I was applying my skills as an entrepreneur to just two projects: writing books like this one and running Threshold 360 as CEO. Today, I apply my broad one thing even more narrowly, spending nearly all my time launching content products like the one you hold in your hand.*

Your one thing may be broad like mine or specific like Bob the piano tuner's. Either is perfectly fine, so long as you are on the focused path to mastering your one thing in order to best glorify God and love your neighbors as yourself. With this in mind, it's now time to look more closely at the characteristics we should be looking for in our one thing, regardless of how broad or specific it turns out to be.

---

* For more examples of the broad and specific "one things" of the masters profiled throughout this book, download the free "Master of One Notebook" at jordanraynor.com/MOO.

THREE QUESTIONS

In my previous book *Called to Create,* I share three questions that some of the most exceptional Christian professionals ask when discerning their calling. As I've interviewed the sources for this book, these questions came up time and time again, making me increasingly confident that these are the best questions to ask in the process of choosing your one vocational thing:

- What am I passionate about?
- What gifts has God given me?
- Where do I have the best opportunity to glorify God and serve others?

These three questions serve as an excellent filter with which to sift through the dozens of different career opportunities many of us are presented with. In my experience, and in the experience of the masters chronicled in this book, it is at the intersection of our passions, gifts, and opportunities that we find our calling—our one thing—the work we can choose to do most masterfully well for the glory of God and the good of others. Although the above questions appear to be straightforward and simple, in reality there is quite a bit of nuance to them that we must understand before we begin our journey to choosing the one thing we will master vocationally.

Passions

One of my favorite books on what it takes to become truly masterful at any one thing is *Grit* by the renowned psychologist Angela Duckworth. In the book Duckworth argues that it is sheer perseverance (or grit), not raw talent, that is the greatest predictor of mastery in any given field.

But in order to be "gritty" and push through the difficult obstacles to achieve greatness in a chosen career, Duckworth argues, you must be "insatiably curious" about the work you are doing. In other words, you must be passionate about your one thing in order to become masterful at it. As Duckworth wrote, "Passion is as necessary as perseverance to world-class excellence."[2]

As we saw in chapter 1, Cal Newport found that passion *follows* mastery, not the other way around. It is only when we get really good at something that we develop passion that is sustainable over a long period of time. How can Newport and Duckworth both be right? Aren't these ideas at odds with each other? Not at all.

When most people seek to discern their calling, they ask *only* the passion question, believing that if they find a job that matches their preexisting passions, they will find near instantaneous happiness and satisfaction that will sustain them long enough to become masterful at their one thing. As we've already seen, this passion hypothesis is simply not true. But that doesn't mean that passion is totally irrelevant. More often than not, passions and preexisting interests serve as signposts pointing the way to the work we are uniquely gifted to do. This is the natural and insatiable curiosity Duckworth refers to as a necessary driver to mastery.

> It is only when we find work that we can do exceptionally well in service of others that we will find deep happiness and passion that is sustainable over the course of our careers.

So, while Newport is right in concluding that identifying our passions is not the end of our search for our one thing, the passion question is still a very helpful place to start. Why? Because God has created each of us with certain passions and interests, and understanding them can be incredibly useful in identifying clues as to which work we might do exceptionally well. And *that* is ultimately what we are looking for: the one thing we can do most extraordinarily well for God's glory and the good of others.

Any time we look exclusively inward to discern our calling, we are doomed to self-doubt and disappointment because this is simply not how God designed us to work. You and I are made in the image of Christ—the ultimate example of service and love. It is only when we find work that we can do exceptionally well in service of others that we will find deep happiness and passion that is sustainable over the course of our careers—the type of passion that leads to grit and mastery.

I have two girls under the age of four, so needless to say, my entire home and world are consumed by Disney princesses. All throughout our house are princess dresses, movies, stuffed animals, and more stickers than you can possibly imagine.* Lately, we have all become big fans of Disney's *Moana*—the story of a teenage princess who sets sail on an adventurous ocean voyage in search of her identity, purpose, and calling. The climax of her journey is marked with—you guessed it—an unforgettable song,† in which Moana appears to have figured it all out. Wide-eyed with revelation, Moana sings, "And the call isn't out there at all, it's inside me."[3]

I *love* this song, and I sing it with gusto along with my kids. But unfortunately, Moana isn't quite right. Calling isn't something we can discover on our own by simply identifying our passions and interests. It's not something buried inside us that we unearth through deep

---

* Seriously, though, the cost to joy ratio on Disney-branded stickers and Band-Aids is off the charts.

† Written by the inimitable Lin-Manuel Miranda.

introspection. Calling—or, in the language of this book, our one thing—is discovered by taking inventory of our interests and applying them in the real world where our work comes in contact with those we are called to serve. Our work can only be a calling if someone calls us to it, and we work for their agenda rather than our own. For the Christian, this means working for the sake of our Savior. What is his agenda? To glorify God and love our neighbors as ourselves. As we saw in the previous two chapters, the way we accomplish this is by doing the best work we can. And we can only identify that work when we go beyond the passion question to focus on our gifts and where we can be of greatest service to others.

Gifts

Just as each of us has different interests and passions, we all have been given different gifts by our heavenly Father. The apostle Paul explained:

> But each has his own gift from God, one of one kind and one of another. (1 Corinthians 7:7, ESV)

> We have different gifts, according to the grace given to each of us. (Romans 12:6)

> Now there are varieties of gifts, but the same Spirit; and there are varieties of service, but the same Lord; and there are varieties of activities, but it is the same God who empowers them all in everyone. To each is given the manifestation of the Spirit for the common good. (1 Corinthians 12:4–7, ESV)

While Scripture makes clear that we all have been given unique gifts, I fear we too often ignore these verses, spending more time envying the gifts of others rather than cultivating our own. If we desire to use our work to glorify God and love our neighbors, we ought to be on a quest to find the work we are most gifted at and focus on doing more and more of that one thing. But as we will see in the next chapter, this takes a lot of experimentation. Early in your career it's tough to know what you will be gifted at until you start putting those gifts to the test in the real world. As we start this journey of choosing and mastering our one thing, it is critical to remember this: it is giftedness—not primarily preexisting passion—that is at the heart of what we are looking for in our calling.

In the next chapter we will take a more practical look at how to identify our gifts, but for now, let this truth sink in: the path to finding work we love starts with seeking work through which we can love others well. If you are looking for work you can be passionate about over a long period of time, spend less time worrying about your preexisting passions and much more time

> **The path to finding work we love starts with seeking work through which we can love others well.**

figuring out which work you're disproportionately gifted at. Rather than focusing primarily on your happiness, focus on finding the work you can do to be of most value to others.

Opportunities

In addition to discerning our passions and gifts, there's a third piece of the puzzle that comprises our one thing: opportunity. While the passion and giftedness questions may be helpful in eliminating dozens of career options, it is likely that without a third question, you will still be left with a crippling number of options to choose from. When I have been faced with multiple paths that appear to marry my passions and gifts, I have found it tremendously helpful to ask which path will give me the greatest opportunity to love and serve others. This is perhaps the most difficult question to answer, as it forces us to become attuned to where God is moving around us, opening and closing doors through which we can marry our passions and gifts and find the deep satisfaction of vocation.

Early in her career my mother-in-law, Sheila, had a number of different jobs, all leveraging her considerable talents as a musician. She played the organ at church. She gave piano lessons from her home. She taught music at an elementary school. But the role she loved most was leading the children's choir at her church. Over the years she developed a great passion and giftedness in leading the children's program, so much so that when she and my father-in-law made the move to another church in town, she dreamed of being able to focus on leading a children's choir program full time. To her surprise, when she went to meet with the church's director of worship, he told her that he had been praying for someone to approach him about that exact job. Without the Lord moving in this way, my mother-in-law wouldn't have had the opportunity to combine her passions and gifts for children's choir in this role (one that she has now been mastering for nearly thirty years).

The role of prayer in the process of identifying opportunities like these cannot be overstated. But it's not simply "open and closed doors" we need to be looking for as we ask the opportunity question; we also need to consider the relative sustainability of our options as we choose our one thing. For most of us, our work is the sole source of income for our families and us. Thus, in order for us to be able to spend years getting masterfully good at our one thing, we must choose work that pays well enough to be sustainable over a long period of time. For example, let's say you're passionate about underwater basket weaving and you are gifted at that obscure craft. If you are the primary breadwinner for your family, it's unlikely that underwater basket weaving is going to be the one thing that you can spend forty plus hours getting masterful at every week. There simply isn't a large enough market willing to pay money for those skills. The reality is that most of us cannot get masterfully good at something if the economics of our chosen one thing are unsustainable.

I once heard advice to the effect that when confronted with different career paths, you should "do what people will pay for." At first this advice made me grimace. As a follower of Christ, money isn't a primary driver for me in my pursuit of excellent work. However, over time I have come to see that this advice is actually quite helpful when it comes to choosing your one thing. Why? Because doing what people will pay for means your one thing is sustainable. More importantly, whether or not somebody will pay for something is usually a good objective measure of how much value you are adding to the world and how well you are serving others through your work.

There's a great scene at the end of the movie *Moneyball* that illustrates this well. Billy Beane, the general manager of the Oakland Athletics (whose creative use of data and spreadsheets turned around the losing team) had just returned from Boston where he received an offer to manage the prestigious Boston Red Sox. Once back in Oakland, Beane shares the dollar figure of the offer with his colleague Peter Brand, to which Brand replies, "That makes you the highest paid [general manager] in the history of sports." Beane doesn't seem to care. "So what?" he replies. "You know, I made one decision in my life based on money, and I swore I would never do it again." Brand then looks at his friend and says, "You're not doing it for the money. You're doing it for what the money says."[4] For Beane, being offered the highest-paying general manager job in the history of sports said that he was masterful at his craft and that he served his owners, players, employees, and fans well through his work.

> **Our one thing ought to be where our passions and gifts collide with the greatest opportunity to love and serve others through masterful work.**

My point here is not that we should chase whichever job will pay us the most. The point is that when searching for opportunities that marry our passions and gifts, we ought to choose work that is sustainable, productive, and useful to our neighbors. In other words, our one thing ought to be where our passions and gifts collide with the greatest opportunity to love and serve others through masterful work.

The Sower and the Seed

What does it look like when our passions, gifts, and opportunities intersect? In other words, how do we know when we have found the one thing we ought to choose to sink our teeth into? The best picture I have found for what this looks like comes from Jesus's parable of the sower in the gospel of Mark.

> Listen! A farmer went out to sow his seed. As he was scattering the seed, some fell along the path, and the birds came and ate it up. Some fell on rocky places, where it did not have much soil.

It sprang up quickly, because the soil was shallow. But when the sun came up, the plants were scorched, and they withered because they had no root. Other seed fell among thorns, which grew up and choked the plants, so that they did not bear grain. Still other seed fell on good soil. It came up, grew and produced a crop, some multiplying thirty, some sixty, some a hundred times. (4:3–8)

Just a few verses later, Jesus explained to his disciples that in this parable "the farmer sows the word" (verse 4:14), showing us how different presentations of God's Word bear different fruit depending on how and where the seeds are sown. As Andy Crouch points out in his excellent book *Culture Making*, this is essentially "a parable about parables—an explanation of the whole parable-telling strategy."[5] What Crouch means by this is that parables are a lot like seeds, in that the sower must be liberal in scattering them to large and diverse crowds in hopes that their truths will take root in the hearts of a few of those listening. Viewed in that light, Jesus's words not only offer us insight into how his Word is received, but they also provide a beautiful picture of how we should think about finding and focusing on our calling. As Crouch explains:

The parable of the prodigal sower is first of all about Jesus' own ministry strategy. But it also applies very closely to the work of culture making. Parables, after all, are cultural goods—new ways of making something of the world. The teller of parables faces the same risks every culture maker does: the risk of seeing the cultural goods we propose flatly rejected, seeing initial enthusiasm and success wither into nothing, or perhaps worst,

seeing our cultural goods survive but not thrive, bearing none
of the fruit we had hoped for or even being turned against their
original purpose. A farmer can inspect and prepare the soil,
but no one has enough power to assure that much of his or her
culture making will not fall onto bad soil. What we can do,
however, is pay careful attention to the fruit of our cultural
work.[6]

Much like the seed that fell along the path, some of our attempts to
discover our one thing will fail right from the start. Maybe you want a
job but don't get an interview. Or maybe you launched a blog that's getting next to no traction. I know I have launched my fair share of projects that failed right out of the gate. A few years ago, in an effort to
inject some creativity into our date nights, my wife and I decided to
date each other "through the alphabet," planning a series of activities
that all started with the same letter. We planned activities starting with
the letter *A* on the first date (arts and crafts, dinner at Acropolis, and
watching *The Avengers*), *B* on the second date, and so on. We had a
blast doing it, and some of our friends tried the idea with great success,
leading Kara and me to believe that there was an opportunity to sell
ideas for these dates in an email subscription product we called #Date-
ThroughZ. It took us just a few days to launch a website, but after
spending a few hundred dollars on Facebook ads without generating a
single customer, we knew the project was a failure.

Most of our attempts to find our calling aren't total failures from
the get-go though. Much of the seed we sow in an attempt to discover
our one thing falls along rocky or thorny soil where fruit "springs up
quickly" only to wither and die over time. This was my experience with
a startup early in my career. My cofounders and I worked tirelessly

building our business, and our diligence was met with quick results. We were signing up customers, getting lots of high-profile press, and raising a bit of venture capital, but the business never bore exponential fruit. Instead, it slowly withered until its eventual death.

While some of our professional exploration will bear resemblance to the seeds sown along the path, the rocky soil, and the thorns, with enough sowing and discerning, at least one of our seeds is bound to land in good soil. Like the farmer, it is here that we will find the early signs of "divine multiplication," with the ground bearing fruit "thirty, sixty and a hundredfold beyond what we could expect from our feeble inputs."[7] Throughout my career as an entrepreneur, I have sown many seeds in an attempt to find the most fertile soil in which to pour my time and energy. In all that experimentation I have experienced this sense of true divine multiplication only once, with the release of my previous book, *Called to Create*. Yes, I have had many successes as an entrepreneur outside that project, but all that fruit was somewhat proportional to the amount of effort I put into the endeavor. But with my book, the results every step along the way were exponentially more than I could ever take credit for in my own strength and abilities. From how easy it was to write, to how well the book has sold long after its initial release, I have had the great joy of stepping back and thanking the Lord for good soil—soil that he has clearly carved out for me to water, plant, and cultivate for his glory and the good of others.

As you begin the search for the one thing you will choose to master in your work, be on the lookout for the early signs of divine multiplication. Just like a crop, the miracle of divine multiplication is not seen overnight. But week by week, month by month, you should begin to see your seeds sprout, your sprouts blossom, and, over time, your blossoms produce fruit at a rate that can only be explained by the grace of God.

Once you've found the soil that appears most likely to produce that kind of fruit, steward it well by pouring all you have into it. It wouldn't make much sense if, after viewing the fruits of the initial sowing, the farmer in Jesus's parable chose to sow more seeds along the path, on the rocky soil, and in the thorns. After reaping the fruits of the good soil, any wise and responsible farmer would focus intensely on cultivating the most productive plot of land. Similarly, once you find the good soil in your own career—the spot where your passions, gifts, and opportunities are beginning to produce significant fruit—it is your responsibility to develop and nurture that soil, pursuing mastery of the work the Lord has created you to do. Crouch summarizes this well:

> The right question is whether, when we undertake the work we believe to be our vocation, we experience the joy and humility that come only when God multiplies our work so that it bears thirty, sixty and a hundredfold beyond what we could expect from our feeble inputs. *Vocation*—calling—becomes another word for a continual process of discernment, examining the fruits of our work to see whether they are producing that kind of fruit, and doing all we can to scatter the next round of seed in the most fruitful places.[8]

THE PROCESS

Now that we know what we are looking for in our one thing, what is the process by which we go about choosing it? It's important to note that the process of discerning one's calling is so nuanced that it can look quite different from person to person. As with many other things in life, our gracious heavenly Father gives us a great deal of freedom and discernment as we seek out the work we will choose to master. There is no one-size-fits-all formula. With that being said, after interviewing dozens of Christians who are unequivocal masters of their crafts and who view their work as a calling from God, I have observed a general process that has proven to be an effective method of discerning one's vocation. Not only have I seen this process work in the lives of others, but I have also found it to be true in my own path to mastery. Over the next four chapters, we will dive deep into each of the four steps along the path to choosing and mastering the work God has called us to do with excellence: Explore, Choose, Eliminate, and Master.

In chapter 5 ("Explore"), we will start down the path to mastery by forming hypotheses about what we think our one thing might be and putting those hypotheses to the test in a process of rapid experimentation. The goal in this first step is—to extend the metaphor of the sower—to gather and scatter seeds widely in an attempt to see what will start to grow.

In chapter 6 ("Choose"), we will examine the fruits of our experimentation and make the difficult decision to "pivot" our careers or "persevere," choosing to commit to developing the one plot of land that is starting to produce the fruits of divine multiplication.

In chapter 7 ("Eliminate"), we will examine why, once you've chosen your one thing, it is essential to eliminate the nonessential, refusing to plant more seeds in the rocky and thorny soil.

Finally, in chapter 8 ("Master"), we will examine the difference between those who are merely good at their jobs and those who are masters of their crafts, deliberately developing the soil in which their one thing is planted through apprenticeships, purposeful practice, and discipline over time.

Are you ready to find the work God put you on this earth to do? If you've already found your one thing, are you prepared to get more focused and more masterful at your vocation? If so, let us start down the path to mastery together!

———————

Chapter Summary

There are likely many things that God has equipped you to do masterfully well in your work. A key to becoming a master of one is making the best possible choice of which one thing you will sink your teeth into vocationally. There are three questions to ask while on the path to finding your one thing: (1) What am I passionate about? (2) What gifts has God given me? (3) Where do I have the best opportunity to glorify God and serve others? It is at the intersection of the answers to these three questions that you are most likely to find the work you were created to do.

Key Scripture

"Few things are needed—or indeed only one" (Luke 10:42).

Next Action

Spend some time writing down the passions, gifts, and opportunities the Lord has revealed to you to date.

Chapter 5

Explore

You rarely have time for everything you want in this life, so you need to make choices. And hopefully your choices can come from a deep sense of who you are.

FRED ROGERS

As the CEO of Simplified, Emily Ley helps busy women simplify their lives through a collection of products. Most notable among them is *The Simplified Planner,* which has been sold hundreds of thousands of times online and in more than eight hundred retail outlets worldwide. "I love my work," Ley shared.[1] "I love being able to create products for women that help them get back to what matters—to the people and the things that really bring them to life."[2]

Ley has found what we're all looking for: an opportunity to do work we love by combining our passions and gifts in a way that impacts others and produces fruit that can only be explained by the grace of God. But before you envy Ley's discovery of her calling, you may be encouraged to learn that it took a long time for her to find her one thing. In fact, Ley's career started with a tremendous amount of insecurity about ever finding work worth committing to.

"Do you remember what it was like to be fresh out of high school, on the cusp of adulthood? When anything could happen? When we stood at the starting lines of our grown-up lives with seemingly hundreds of roads to choose from? . . . I wouldn't go back there if you paid me!" Ley said.[3] Like so many of us today, Ley's career started with a seemingly limitless number of options that were at once exhilarating and paralyzing. Ley felt overwhelmed by the number of different paths her career could take. Her frustration was compounded by the fact that she had many friends who seemed to know exactly what they wanted to be (doctors, accountants, lawyers, teachers) and whose paths to mastering their one thing were crystal clear. "I, however, had absolutely no idea what I wanted to do with my life," Ley remembered. "All I knew was that I wanted the chance to be creative. I wanted to inspire people and make an impact. I wanted to be challenged and pushed."[4]

In short, Ley was looking for where her passions and gifts as a creative person could come together to love and serve others extraordinarily well. But she had no idea which road would lead to her discovering and choosing her one thing. So what did she do? She did what almost every other master in this book did at one point in their careers: she formed hypotheses about the work she thought might be her thing, and she put those hypotheses to the test by exploring a myriad of different options.

"I shadowed family friends at work. I visited my mom's classroom. I even majored in education for a few short months . . . and changed my major to English," Ley explained.[5] But none of those career options seemed like the right fit. "I stood looking out at my options, and I felt heavy with worry. None of the roads looked like the one I felt God was paving in my heart. None felt right for me."[6] Even after college Ley still didn't feel she had a clear sense of where God was calling her to work, so she decided to venture off into the corporate world. "While I had a few great jobs and incredible titles, I never felt I'd found the right fit. It felt like something was missing," Ley said.

Somewhere along the way, Ley became interested in graphic design. One day she decided to take a small risk and experiment with launching a shop on Etsy to sell stationery and digital monograms. "As I googled a million questions and watched all the YouTube tutorials I could get my hands on, I taught myself to be a graphic designer," she shared. While keeping her corporate day job, Ley "used every millisecond of spare time" to start building her business. "I worked in the middle of the night, many evenings until 2 a.m., before a 6 a.m. alarm sounded the start of another day at my corporate job."[7]

Ley had found creative work that she was gifted at (as evidenced by her rapidly growing business), and as her business grew, her passion for the work followed suit, causing her to work late into the night. But she didn't ditch her corporate job at the first sign of success of her nascent business. Instead, Ley spent two years getting great at her craft, building a financial runway for her business, and placing incremental bets on her side hustle. She took the time to properly explore and experiment with this increasingly promising option for the one thing she could master professionally. "Every morning, I'd trade my self-taught Illustrator skills for Excel spreadsheets. I'd swap my topknot and highlighter-covered hands for a skirt suit. But I knew, deep in my heart, that God had a calling for me," Ley recalled. "And the harder I worked and the more I tiptoed down that path, the clearer God made it. And little by little, mistake by mistake, milestone after milestone, I built a business. God took my itty-bitty dream to build a better life for myself and my family, and he grew it into what is now a major brand of simple day planners, baby books, and home-office accessories sold worldwide."[8]

If Ley hadn't been willing to take time to explore different career options (including teaching, corporate America, and graphic design), she might have never found the one

> **The path to finding and focusing on your one thing is often messy, creative, and fueled by a healthy dose of exploration and experimentation.**

thing that has brought her the satisfaction of vocation and the opportunity to serve hundreds of thousands of women. The stories of Ley and the other masters in this book illustrate an important point for us to consider as we start down the path to mastery together: The path to finding and focusing on your one thing is rarely direct. More often than not, it is messy, creative, and fueled by a healthy dose of exploration and experimentation.

In his book *Essentialism,* Greg McKeown contrasts what he calls "Essentialists" and their "Nonessentialist" counterparts. If you are tracking with the case I have been building throughout this book, you are an Essentialist, believing that the path to producing our most excellent work is "going big" on one thing vocationally. Here's what McKeown has to say about Essentialists and the importance of exploring and experimenting with many different career options:

> One paradox of Essentialism is that Essentialists actually explore more options than their Nonessentialist counterparts. Nonessentialists get excited by virtually everything and thus react to everything. But because they are so busy pursuing every opportunity and idea they actually explore less. The way of the Essentialist, on the other hand, is to explore and evaluate a broad set of options before committing to any. Because Essentialists will commit and "go big" on only the vital few ideas or activities, they explore more options at first to ensure they pick the right one later.[9]

The path to finding and focusing on the one vocational thing we will master starts with intentionally exploring our options. But before we can begin experimenting with different opportunities, we must take the time to form hypotheses about what we think our one thing might be—where our passions and gifts might intersect to be of the utmost use to those around us.

Forming "One Thing" Hypotheses

The best way to start forming these hypotheses is by submitting the pursuit of your calling to the Lord in prayer. Trying to find your one vocational thing can feel daunting and cause great anxiety. But Jesus has invited us to cast those anxieties upon him (see 1 Peter 5:7). For while the burden of discerning our calling may seem heavy to us, it is light as a feather to him (see Matthew 11:30). In Proverbs 16:3, we read the following promise: "Commit your work to the Lord, and your plans will be established" (ESV). We commit our work to the Lord when we commit ourselves to the pursuit of excellent work that will reveal God's character to the world and love our neighbors as ourselves. If you haven't already, take a moment right now to go to the Lord in prayer and ask him to direct your steps (see Psalm 119:133) along the path to mastery, guiding you to the work that you can choose to do masterfully well for his glory and the good of others.

Once you've asked the Lord to reveal where your passions and gifts intersect with opportunities to love and serve others through your work, it is time to ask similar questions of yourself in order to start forming some hypotheses of what you think your one thing might be. Understanding who you are and how God has made you is a critical step in this process. If you are at the beginning of your career (or are looking to start down the path to mastery anew), try answering the following questions in order to better articulate your personal narrative. The answers to these questions can serve as insightful signposts pointing the way to the work that might best combine your passions and gifts:

- Which life events have had the biggest impact in shaping who you are?
- What makes you different from those around you?

- What things are you naturally curious about today?
- Which activities did you naturally gravitate toward when you were younger?
- What do you find yourself daydreaming about when nothing else is commanding your attention?
- Who are your role models?
- What about their lives and careers do you respect and want to see modeled in your own life?
- Is there a common thread that connects all of your current or past vocational interests?

If you have some professional experience under your belt, ask yourself the following questions as well:

- Which work have you excelled at historically?
- When have you felt the most alive and useful in your career?
- Where have you seen the fruits of "divine multiplication" in your work?

Answering these questions at the start of your path to mastery can be instrumental in helping you speed up the rate at which you are able to choose your one thing. For example, if I had explored these questions while in college, it is likely that I would have identified my entrepreneurial tendencies much sooner than I did. Asking myself a question such as "Which activities did you naturally gravitate toward when you were younger?" would have helped me recognize that as a kid I was always working to build some type of business, whether it was a baseball-card shop in my bedroom or selling carnations door-to-door for a school fund-raiser. Taking the time early in my career to identify these important moments in my story would likely have helped me discern and choose my one thing earlier in life. Take the time to read your own personal narrative. In the words of the ancient Greek poet Pindar, "Become who you are by learning who you are."

In addition to this important step of introspection, it is critical that we spend time asking others where they believe our passions and gifts might intersect to form a calling. After all, the primary characteristic we are looking for in our one thing is where we can be of the utmost use and service to others, so it makes sense to begin seeking feedback from others early on the path to mastery. Ask your family, friends, spouse, customers, bosses, and colleagues what they believe you are truly exceptional at. Don't let them off the hook with vague generalities. Seek direct feedback about the specific work they believe you can do most masterfully well. Throughout this process be sure to give particular weight to the feedback from other Christians who are filled with the Holy Spirit, as this is one of the most powerful and direct ways the Lord speaks to us as we strive to discern our one thing (see Matthew 10:20).

––––––––

If my friend Christy Adams had listened only to her "inner voice" without seeking input from other believers, she may never have found her calling. Adams grew up wanting to be a zookeeper, but that dream quickly took a back seat to her interest in ophthalmology. As a child, Adams had a number of conditions related to her sight, which forced her to have multiple medical procedures conducted on her eyes. This sparked an interest to become a doctor so she could help others like herself. "I thought it would be cool to give people the gift of sight. I thought it was life changing," Adams remembered. But after a brief internship with an ophthalmologist while she was in high school, Adams quickly realized that wasn't the work she wanted to commit her life to. "The day-to-day work of being an ophthalmologist is actually kind of gross. I would go into this office, sit with the doctors, and it seemed like all they did was deal with a lot of disgusting eye juice. Clearly, this wasn't for me. But I'm so glad I had that experience because it saved me from going further down that career path."[10]

Like so many young people fresh out of high school, Adams entered college with little idea of what she wanted to do with her life. Prayer and introspection alone were not clarifying her calling. Clearly there was a missing piece to the puzzle of discerning her one thing. As Adams explained, that missing piece was listening to the feedback of others—in particular, other Christians—that put her on the path to mastery.

"While in school at the University of Georgia, I signed up to go on a summer missions trip to Mexico with my church," Adams shared. "Just before the trip, one of the members of our group volunteered me to serve as a translator."[11] Adams had only two years of experience learning Spanish in high school, but her fellow church members noticed that she had an unusual aptitude for the language, so they suggested she put those gifts to the test.

That missions trip proved to be a crucial step on Adams's path to finding her one vocational thing. Once in Mexico she discovered that she loved teaching English to Spanish speakers and vice versa, and over the next few years, her giftedness and passion for that work grew simultaneously. Adams—whose early professional interests were as broad as ophthalmology, zoology, and broadcast journalism—has spent her entire fourteen-year postcollegiate career mastering her role as a middle school Spanish teacher, a career she believes the Lord has clearly called her to. But she may never have found her one thing if she hadn't examined her own interests as well as what others suggested she might be gifted at. Through this process Adams formed a number of hypotheses about what her one thing might be. But it was only after she put those hypotheses to the test that she was able to move further down the path to mastery.

THE FIVE PRINCIPLES OF EFFECTIVE EXPERIMENTATION

Once you've taken the time to identify your interests and ask others which work they think you might have a propensity for, it's likely that you will have an extensive list of ideas of what your one vocational thing might be.* This is an exciting place to be, but a list of possible vocations is not of much value in and of itself. It is only when we, like Adams and Ley, put these hypotheses to the test that we start to make serious progress in finding our one thing. In the words of *Grit* author Angela Duckworth, "The process of [vocational] discovery can be messy, serendipitous, and inefficient. This is because you can't really predict with certainty what will capture your attention and what won't. . . . Without experimenting, you can't figure out which interests will stick, and which won't."[12]

But what does this process of experimentation look like? How do we experiment with our potential callings while ensuring we don't wind up ten years down the road as a master of none? In my research, interviews for this book, and my own personal experience, I have observed five principles of effective experimentation that will help you make the most of this important step on the path to mastery.

Place Little Bets

First, whenever possible, place little bets when experimenting with what you think your one thing might be. This can be done through

---

* You can keep track of these hypotheses in the "Master of One Notebook," which you can download for free at jordanraynor.com/MOO.

short-term internships, side hustles that you take on in addition to your nine-to-five job, or projects at your current job that fall outside your formal job description.

When Emily Ley became interested in starting a graphic design business, she didn't immediately quit her corporate job. She formed a hypothesis about what she thought she might be gifted at and placed her first little bet: teaching herself the basics of graphic design via You-Tube tutorials. As that started to bear fruit, she placed a slightly bigger bet by selling her first five-dollar products on Etsy. Over time, the size of Ley's bets grew in correlation with her confidence that building a business around her designs was the one thing she wanted to master.

Similarly, Christy Adams placed her first little bet when she agreed to serve as a translator on her church's mission trip to Mexico. At the time, Adams had no idea that this little bet would end up being the nudge that pushed her down the path to a career mastering the art of teaching Spanish. But that's exactly the point of placing little bets. When you're at the beginning of the path to mastery, you want to place as many smart little bets as you can, as it is nearly impossible to predict which of those little bets will pay off and start to show signs that your one thing is taking shape.

Embrace Being a Jack-or-Jill-of-All-Trades

You read that right. Just a few dozen pages after I opened this book passionately calling you and me *not* to be jacks-and-jills-of-all-trades and masters of none, here I am telling you that being a jack-of-all-trades can actually play an important role at the start of the path to mastering your one thing. Here's why: in order to make the best choice about the work in which you are going to pursue mastery for years and maybe even decades, it is a wise and valuable use of time to explore as many options as you can before committing to any one of them. At this stage in your career, your one thing should be exploring as many potential vocations as possible.

Remember that comically long list of career options my roommates and I developed when I was in college? In the first few years of my career, I put many of those hypotheses to the test in a series of little bets to try to find my one thing. When I was at Florida State, I worked for a statewide political party; took classes in public relations, political science, and music; had a summer job selling newspaper subscriptions; played keyboard in an alternative

> **Risk should be celebrated and fear of failure should be minimized, so long as you are making excellent, fast, and inexpensive missteps.**

rock/emo band at gigs throughout Florida;* and spent a year waking up at five o'clock in the morning to work part time for a tech startup. When I graduated, I was the quintessential jack-of-all-trades and master of none, but due to my rapid experimentation, I had a much clearer idea of what my one thing would (and would not) be, which allowed me to make better, more informed decisions about my career.

Fail Fast

In tech startup culture, failure is somewhat celebrated due to the tremendous learning opportunities it can provide. Your product didn't work in one market? Better to know you've failed now than just before you run out of financial runway six months from now. Likewise, when we are exploring various options to discover what our one thing might

---

* Believe it or not.

be, failure can provide a lot of valuable information about which work we are not gifted at and thus are unlikely to do masterfully well for the glory of God and the good of others. At this stage on the path to mastery, risk should be celebrated and fear of failure should be minimized, so long as you are making excellent, fast, and inexpensive missteps. Matt Perman articulates this well:

> You learn by trying things and making mistakes. This isn't contrary to the point about doing what you do with excellence. It means that, when making a decision about next steps, sometimes you might find you were wrong, and this can be an advantage in the long run because of the knowledge you will have gained from the experience. You sought to make that decision with excellence, but it turned out not to have been the best decision. You couldn't have known that before. As with everything, so with mistakes: make excellent mistakes. Make mistakes of forward motion, not mistakes of sloth. Try things, be bold, and see what happens.[13]

Go Where You Will Learn the Most

When I decided to bring my first books to market, I placed a couple of little bets, self-publishing two titles and teaching myself how to market and sell books on my own. To my surprise, these books did well—not "divine multiplication" well, but well enough to convince me to place bigger and bigger bets on my writing. When I got the idea for *Called to Create,* I knew the book would appeal to a much wider audience than my first two did. My initial instinct was to self-publish, knowing that on a per-unit basis, I would earn a much higher royalty than if I signed a deal with a traditional publisher.

But as my agent and I started having conversations with major publishers who were interested in acquiring the rights to publish the book, it became very clear very quickly that I had *a lot* to learn about how to write and sell a book on a massive scale. It was also clear that, while I could probably learn those things on my own, I would learn exponentially faster by partnering with a traditional publisher who would also serve as a relatively objective third party, providing me with valuable feedback on whether or not I should continue to invest in writing as opposed to other entrepreneurial endeavors. Knowing that it might mean sacrificing greater short-term income, I signed a deal with a major publishing house and banked on the fact that what I would learn through that experience would pay off even bigger dividends over time.

Now, I can say emphatically that the bet paid off. My experience working with traditional publishers has made me a much better writer and marketer while giving me a depth of knowledge of the publishing industry that would have taken me years, maybe even a decade, to figure out on my own.

One of my friends has a piece of advice he gives people who are trying to decide between two professional paths: "Go where you will learn the most." I love this advice for any stage of your career, but especially as you are in the stage of exploring and experimenting with what you think your one thing might be. I always advise people in this stage to, whenever possible, prioritize speed of learning over short-term income when you are still trying to discern your calling. The more quickly you learn, the sooner you will be able to choose the work you can do masterfully well.

Keep Your One Thing in Mind

The fifth and final principle of effective experimentation is to keep your one thing in mind at all times. As you are putting your hypotheses to the test via side-hustle businesses, projects, internships, and part-time jobs, remind yourself that all this experimentation is a means to an end: identifying the one thing that best combines your passions and gifts in a clear opportunity to serve others through masterful work. Remember, it is not being a jack-or-jill-of-all-trades that is problematic. It is when we fail to become a master of one that we squander our God-given passions and gifts that are meant to be poured out as an offering to the world. After starting the path to mastery with our one thing in mind, we need to be sure to keep that goal in sight, to be constantly on the lookout for where in our experimental scattering of seeds things are starting to take root, grow, and show the early signs of divine multiplication.

Before they planted the first seeds of what would grow to become Monday Night Brewing, the company's founders—Jeff Heck, Joel Iverson, and Jonathan Baker—were simply three young, ambitious men whose friendship quickly developed through the weekly Bible study they attended together. On one Monday night (the only night all three friends had free that week), they decided to get together with some other Bible study friends to try out a fifty-dollar beer-making kit that Heck had received from his wife. That first Monday night brewing session quickly grew into a weekly ritual, with the three friends getting together to experiment with new recipes. In the words of the friends who are now his business partners, Heck displayed "an anal-retentive passion for perfection" in pursuit of brewing the most excellent beer. That pursuit of masterful brewing led to an ever-growing group of friends who would stop by Heck's garage on Monday nights to sample the latest experimental brews. This weekly cycle went on for five years before Heck and his friends decided it was time to turn their hobby into a business, officially catapulting Monday Night Brewing out of Heck's garage and into the market. But what's more interesting than the process of experimenting with different beer recipes is how Heck (now Monday Night Brewing's CEO) experimented with his career until he chose the one thing he was going to master.

As Heck explained, "When I graduated from Harvard in 2003, I had no idea what I wanted to do. I was trying to decide between going to medical school, going to seminary, taking my band on the road, or going and working for a large corporation. I was a train wreck when it came to focus." Heck ended up following the "go where you will learn the most" principle, taking a job at Atlanta-based Home Depot in a program that allowed promising young executives to place little bets working in a variety of the company's different business units in short six-month stints. This allowed Heck to spend a few months working in investor relations, then in operations, and then in a Home Depot retail location, working every job in the store over the course of six months. Eventually, Heck landed in Home Depot's mergers and acquisitions (M&A) team where he settled down for the first few years of his career.

While Heck enjoyed his work helping Home Depot acquire companies, he yearned for more experience helping entrepreneurs build their businesses. So after a few years at Home Depot, Heck left to take a job at a private equity firm where he was able to leverage his M&A skills to acquire controlling interests in a variety of businesses. But unlike at Home Depot, after these investment deals were closed, Heck was able to roll up his sleeves and experiment with his skills as an operator, helping the CEOs of his firm's portfolio companies build organizational structures and systems to help their businesses scale. It didn't take long for Heck to realize that this was the type of work he was created to do. He was getting much closer to his one thing. But in the back of his mind, Heck expected that he would one day apply his skills as an operator to running a single organization of his own.

It was while Heck was working in private equity that he and his Bible study buddies started experimenting with craft beer recipes in Heck's garage. Once the trio officially launched Monday Night Brewing, Heck's two cofounders became the first to leave their well-paying jobs to focus on the brewery full time. But Heck hung back and spent years straddling the responsibilities of his demanding private equity job, his newly founded brewery, and his role as a husband and father of three young kids. "In retrospect, I had way too much on my plate," Heck recalled. "I knew I wanted to dedicate myself fully to building Monday Night, but it didn't make sense for me to make the leap at the time." While Heck was clearly passionate about the business, his gifts as an operator of later-stage businesses simply didn't align with the needs of Monday Night Brewing at that moment in the brewery's life cycle.

But that changed as Monday Night's success started to take off. "We were getting to the point in which we had thirty or forty employees, when, frankly, we needed a little bit more sophistication around analytics and process and culture and scale," Heck explained. "We all recognized that the business was in a position in which I would be able to help move the needle with my skill set." In other words, as the brewery grew, Heck saw an opportunity to combine his passions and gifts in a single direction to love and serve his cofounders, investors, employees, and customers well. Heck made the leap and joined Monday Night Brewing full time as CEO, a role he has held ever since. Today, this former "train wreck of focus" is truly a master of one. Heck and his cofounders are laser focused on building a business that glorifies God and "deepens human relationships through some of the best beer in the country."

As Jeff Heck, Emily Ley, and Christy Adams so powerfully demonstrate, the wisest way to start down the path to becoming a master of one is first to take the time to explore and experiment with the various things we suspect might be our calling. Then, as we examine the fruits of our experiments, seek feedback from others, and in the words of Heck, "observe what the Lord is doing and where he is leading," we will be well on our way to finding the one vocational thing worth choosing to commit to.[14]

Chapter Summary

The path to finding and focusing on your one vocational thing starts with intentionally exploring your options. Once you've formed some ideas about what your one thing might be, it is time to put those hypotheses to the test and experiment with your options to find the work you can do most exceptionally well for God's glory and the good of others. As you go through this process, keep the five principles of effective experimentation in mind: (1) Place little bets. (2) Temporarily embrace being a jack-or-jill-of-all-trades. (3) Fail fast. (4) Go where you will learn the most. (5) Keep your one thing in mind.

Key Scripture

"Commit your work to the LORD, and your plans will be established" (Proverbs 16:3, ESV).

Next Action

If you are still searching for the one thing you will master vocationally, take time to write down some hypotheses about what your one thing might be. If you have already chosen your one thing, write down how you could apply one of the five principles of effective experimentation to the work you are seeking to master.

Chapter 6

Choose

Blessed are the single hearted: (for that is the real meaning of the word we translate "the pure in heart"). If your heart is not wholly in the work, the work will not be good—and work that is not good serves neither God nor the community; it only serves mammon.

DOROTHY SAYERS

A middle-aged man swings open the door and enters his home. He swaps out his sport coat for a cardigan sweater and slips into a pair of blue canvas shoes, all while singing a song. Then he looks straight into the camera and offers a simple greeting: "Hello, neighbor!" This is Fred Rogers, the gentle, soft-spoken man who essentially played himself as the host of *Mister Rogers' Neighborhood*—the beloved educational show that was watched by millions of children between 1968 and 2001.

What is commonly known is that Rogers was a master of his craft, spending decades getting exceptionally good at his work of educating children through the medium of television. What is less known is the winding path Rogers took to choosing his one thing—a journey that spanned many years and saw its fair share of twists and turns.

Rogers had a term he liked to use when referring to discerning one's calling. He called it "guided drift."[1] Guided by what? Dr. Junlei Li, the codirector of the Fred Rogers Center, explained that "Fred was guided by a deep sense of service, of wanting to be useful to the world. He was driven by service even if in his mind it was vague for years as to how to best leverage his considerable talents in service of others."[2] A devout Christian, Rogers deeply understood one of the central themes of this book: that as Christians, the gospel of Jesus's selfless sacrifice should compel us to view our whole lives as service to others. When it comes to our work, the proper response to the gospel is not to seek out the work that will earn us the most fame and fortune. The goal should be to find the work we can do most exceptionally well in service of God and others. In the words of Rogers himself, "You don't set out to be rich and famous; you set out to be helpful."[3] And we are most helpful when we are focused on mastering one thing at a time vocationally. "Deep and simple—that's what matters," Rogers said.[4]

As he was exploring his own path to mastery, Rogers identified many interests and passions, but he was always on the lookout for the one thing that best combined his passions with his considerable gifts to be the most "helpful" to others. As his biographer observed, this deep sense of service came from "the Presbyterian values" instilled by his parents, those of "hard work, responsibility and caring for others, parsimony, duty to family, ethical clarity, a strong sense of mission, and a relentless sense of service to God [that] drove every moment of Fred Rogers's life," including how he thought about discerning his calling.[5]

Rogers grew up in Latrobe, Pennsylvania, just forty miles southeast of Pittsburgh. In material terms, Rogers's upbringing could hardly have been easier. His parents, the unofficial "first couple of Latrobe," were incredibly wealthy and could provide for any of Rogers's needs and then some. But emotionally, Rogers's childhood was challenging. Overweight, frequently ill, and shy, "Fat Freddy" was the target of relentless teasing and ridicule from the other kids in town, leading Rogers to spend much of his childhood hiding away at home. It was there that Rogers spent countless hours playing the piano and escaping to the attic to play with the puppets that would end up becoming central characters in his Neighborhood of Make-Believe. By the time Rogers reached high school, much of the harassment from his peers had stopped, and Rogers grew into his own, confident and focused on his future, even though his path to finding his one vocational thing was far from clear.

Given that "music was the singular passion of Fred's young life," Rogers decided to take his experimentation with the piano to the next level and enrolled in the music composition program at Rollins College north of Orlando, Florida.[6] There, Rogers excelled. He always knew he had a passion for music, and at Rollins he found independent validation from others that he was quite gifted at the craft. But music wasn't the only passion Rogers explored in his collegiate years. His own emotional pain as a child had led him to start studying the field of child development. While "impressed with Fred's musical abilities," Rogers's wife, Joanne (who was enrolled at Rollins with her future husband), "thought he might wind up running an orphanage. He talked about children and their education all the time, and he often went to visit nursery school classes and children's centers to observe the children and their teachers, and to develop his own thoughts on education." Later on "she [remembered] that she had never encountered quite such a focused young man, and that his focus seemed to center around children as well as music."[7]

Upon graduation from Rollins, Rogers still had little idea of what his vocation might be. While he was passionate about music and clearly gifted at the craft of composition, he "had doubts that he could turn his love of music into a career," which was a problem for Rogers who was always looking for where he could be the most helpful and of service to others—especially children.[8] For a long time, Rogers thought the answer might be pastoral ministry, leading to his application and acceptance into Western Theological Seminary (now Pittsburgh Theological Seminary), which he planned to attend after graduating from Rollins. But then Rogers saw television for the first time and his "guided drift" received a major jolt that forever altered the trajectory of his life and the lives of millions of children.

It was Easter break, and Rogers had come home to Latrobe to visit his parents before heading back to Florida for his last few weeks of classes at Rollins. While he was away at school, the family had purchased a television—one of the first in Latrobe. Sitting down at the ten-inch set in the parlor of his parents' mansion, Rogers changed channels until he came across a children's program that caught his attention. What he saw appalled him. As Rogers later recalled, "I saw people dressed in some kind of costumes, literally throwing pies in each other's faces. I was astounded at that."[9] Rogers's first impression of TV was that it was gimmicky and even demeaning. "And if there's anything that bothers me, it's one person demeaning another," Rogers said.[10]

While Rogers "hated" what he saw in that first show, he also instantly appreciated how the medium of television could be used for good, particularly in the education of children. "And I thought: This could be a wonderful tool for education, why is it being used this way? And so I said to my parents, 'You know, I don't think I'll go to seminary right away; I think maybe I'll go into television. . . . Let's see what we can do with this.'"[11]

At first glance Rogers's decision to abandon seminary for television may seem like the impulsive thing you would expect from an unfocused college senior. But as Rogers's biographer explains, the decision was actually quite deliberate:

> Fred Rogers was interested in lots of things: in religion, in becoming a minister, in music composition, in playing the piano, in children and education—and, now, in television production. Because of his well-developed ability to focus

and to think his way over the hurdles he encountered in life, he could envision what television might offer to children and to himself. He understood that the right kind of programming, grounded in a good knowledge of child development, could become a highly inventive and creative way to help young viewers. And he understood that television could give him a unique opportunity to marry his skills in music and entertainment with his interest in children's education. Fred saw that there could be a career opportunity that would blend his aspirations in the more structured field of education with his powerful, more free-form creative instincts. He saw the chance to be both an educator and an artist, and he knew right away that he wanted it.[12]

In other words, Rogers caught a glimpse of what his one thing might be and then made a significant adjustment to his career path in order to pursue it. Rogers wouldn't launch the now-legendary *Mister Rogers' Neighborhood* for another seventeen years after that seminal moment in front of his parents' TV; but throughout those years, Rogers was continually tweaking the direction of his "guided drift" in pursuit of that single opportunity to best combine his passions and gifts in service to others. Then, once he found it, he chose to commit to it and spent decades mastering the art of educating young children in his *Neighborhood*.

During commencement speeches to college graduates, Rogers delighted in talking about his journey down the path to choosing and mastering his one thing. In one such speech, Rogers shared, "I'll never forget the sense of wholeness I felt when I finally realized what in fact I really was: not just a writer or a language buff or a student of human development or a telecommunicator, but I was someone who could use every talent that had ever been given to me in the service of children and their families."[13]

Once we've explored who we are—who God has made us to be and the work he has equipped us to do most exceptionally well—it is essential that we model Rogers's extraordinary focus and intensity, choosing to go big on our one thing and committing to becoming masterful at it in service of God's glory and the good of others.

THE CHOICE

In the world of tech startups, there's a popular idea made famous by Eric Ries's book *The Lean Startup* called a "pivot." The idea goes something like this. Before launching a new product, a good entrepreneur forms clear hypotheses about how the product might solve some problem for a prospective market of customers. Once that product gets into the hands of real customers, the entrepreneur quickly gathers feedback and data that start to either validate or reject the hypotheses. If the product is clearly working and is meeting a need in the market, the entrepreneur will "persevere." But if the product is not working or the market isn't responding as hoped, the entrepreneur may decide to "pivot" the venture, defined in *The Lean Startup* as "a structured course correction designed to test a new fundamental hypothesis about the product, strategy, and engine of growth."[14]

The decision to pivot or persevere is one that startups have to make frequently (as I can personally attest to). But it's not just startups that have to make these difficult calls. On the path to mastery, we are forced to make many left/right decisions—decisions to pivot or persevere in pursuit of the path that best combines our passions and gifts to glorify God and serve others through our work. Take Fred Rogers, for example. When Rogers was a senior in college, he was wrapping up his degree in music composition and planning to pivot his path to pastoral ministry. But once he saw television for the first time, he chose to make a different pivot, parlaying his degree in music composition into a job at NBC where he composed music for the network's shows while simultaneously learning the art of television production. Later in his career Rogers faced a different pivot-or-persevere moment when, shortly after the debut of *The Children's Corner* (the precursor to *Mister Rogers' Neighborhood*) that Rogers helped produce, he was yet again feeling the pull to pastoral ministry. But Rogers recognized that while both were good opportunities to leverage his passions and gifts in service of others, there was clearly a better option for him. Rogers chose to persevere in his work in television, committing the rest of his working life to getting masterful at that one thing.

Each time you go through the process of exploring and experimenting with different work that you believe might be your one thing, you will come to a point at which you know you have enough data, feedback, and insights to make a decision to pivot or persevere. At this point it is time to revisit our three questions:

- What am I passionate about?
- What gifts has God given me?
- Where do I have the best opportunity to glorify God
  and serve others?

Just as you did at the start of this journey, pray over these questions, examine them introspectively, and be sure to discuss them with other followers of Christ. If after your experimentation it's clear that you have yet to find your one thing, it is likely time to pivot.

Pivot

It is important to note that a pivot does not equal failure. Not even close. If you've come to a point at which you decide to pivot and go down a different trail on your path to mastery, it means you have learned more about who you are and the work God has created you to do (and not do). This is something that should be celebrated, not mourned. In the words of John Mark Comer, "It's just as important to know who you're *not* and what you aren't called to, as it is to know who you are and what you *are* called to. Because the clearer your sense of identity and calling are, the more you can focus on what God made you to do."[15]

Not only is pivoting not failure, but more often it is the experience we gain from the thing we are pivoting away from that allows us to pivot one step closer to our calling. Allow me to illustrate this with a personal example. After years of pursuing a career in political campaigns, I spent a semester interning at the White House. While this was an exciting and gratifying experience, my time in Washington helped convince me that politics wasn't going to be the one thing I was willing to commit my career to. So I pivoted from political campaigns to running a political tech startup. Then, as I experimented with that, I realized that I wanted my one thing to be broader than startups in the political space. So I pivoted once again to focus my career on entrepreneurship more generally, applying my skills to launching and supporting the growth of products as diverse as a location data business and full-length nonfiction books like the one you're holding in your hands. There were few skills and experiences wasted in these pivots. On the contrary, the skills I picked up at each turn helped bring me closer and closer to choosing and mastering my one thing. Discussing career pivots in his best-selling book *Mastery,* Robert Greene wrote, "You don't want to abandon the skills and experience you have gained, but to find a new way to apply them. Your eye is on the future, not the past. Often such creative readjustments lead to a superior path for us—we are shaken out of our complacency and forced to reassess where we are headed. Remember: your Life's Task [or, in the vernacular of this book, your one thing] is a living, breathing organism."[16]

Finally, as the story of my childhood friend Josh Eicholtz shows, oftentimes God uses the pivots in our lives to better prepare us for the thing we will eventually choose to master. Unlike most people, Eicholtz knew what his one thing was from an early age, almost from the moment he and I watched a helicopter land in a field behind our middle school classroom. The helicopter was operated by JAARS—a partner of Wycliffe Bible Translators, responsible for flying Bible translators in and out of some of the most remote areas of the world in order to bring the gospel to unreached people groups. School visits like the one Eicholtz and I witnessed are common for JAARS staffers as they attempt to inspire kids to consider a career in mission aviation. In the case of my friend, it worked. Around this same time, Eicholtz had read *Through Gates of Splendor*—the true story of Jim Elliot and four other missionaries (one of whom was a missionary pilot) who were killed in the jungles of Ecuador after taking a risk to bring the gospel to an unreached people group. "The Lord used that book and a helicopter literally flying into my life to start to direct my path," Eicholtz shares. "I felt the Lord calling, and sometime in high school I was like, 'Yeah, *this* is what I want to do with my life.'"

Eicholtz had formed a clear hypothesis about what his one thing might be. To put this hypothesis to the test, he moved to Longview, Texas, to enroll in the highly regarded aviation program at LeTourneau University. As it turned out, Eicholtz was not only passionate about aviation and the idea of becoming a missionary pilot, but he was also quite gifted at the craft. When it came time to graduate, Eicholtz was more certain than ever that mission aviation was the best possible combination of his passions and gifts and the vehicle for him to do his most masterful work. There was just one problem: after spending four years at a private university, he had racked up a tremendous amount of debt—far too much to ask donors to help pay off. "That's when the doubt started creeping in," Eicholtz shares. "I felt like the Lord was clearly calling me to mission aviation, but now, with all this debt, I knew I had to take a detour on my life path."

Eicholtz found something that aligned his passions and gifts, but he didn't yet see an opportunity to apply those things to the work he believed the Lord was calling him to. So he decided to make a pivot in his career, taking a job at Garmin in the firm's aviation department, where he leveraged his skills as a pilot and a computer programmer (skills he picked up in a few classes at LeTourneau) to help build GPS systems for aircraft. This was a fairly significant pivot for Eicholtz, who believed he was being called to work as a missionary pilot in South America or Papua New Guinea. Instead he was going to work every day at the corporate headquarters of Garmin in Olathe, Kansas.

After five years at Garmin, Eicholtz had paid off his debt and joined the team at JAARS. Today he serves as a missionary pilot in Papua New Guinea with his family, working every day to get more masterful at the one thing he sensed the Lord calling him to do since he was a teenager. A lot of people might view their years at a place like Garmin as wasted. But not Eicholtz. As he explains, "Scripture is clear that we are to pursue all of our work with excellence—even if it's not the thing we feel the Lord is calling us to do long term. My years at Garmin helped me pay off my debt and pushed me further down the path to focusing on the work I believed the Lord was calling me to do. But it was also valuable in other ways. In those five years I was able to learn far more about aviation and spend more time honing my skills as a pilot. The Lord used those years to better prepare me for the work I have now chosen to commit myself to overseas."[17]

Persevere

If after realizing that the work you have been experimenting with is the best intersection of your passions, gifts, and opportunities, it may be time to choose to commit to your one thing and persevere down the path to mastery. But before you do, allow me to suggest asking one final question.

I have a personal rule that I will pass on hiring someone unless my team and I can say the person is a "nine or ten" on a ten-point scale measuring how enthusiastic we are that the candidate is the right fit for the job. When you're hiring someone, you are committing to spending thousands of hours working alongside that person, so you want to be sure you make the best possible decision. Even when it's tempting to fill positions as quickly as possible, my team and I try our best to pass on good people in order to save ourselves for the very best. I'd encourage you to apply the same principle to your decisions to pivot or persevere on the path to mastery. If you have reached the point in your journey at which you are prepared to choose your one thing, there's a good chance you will spend years, maybe even decades pursuing mastery of that craft. Can you say this one thing is a nine or a ten? Are you as confident as you reasonably can be that this is the work you can do to best glorify God and love your neighbor as yourself? If the answer is no, it may be time to pivot and keep exploring. If the answer is yes, choose to commit and go all in on your one thing.

Both decisions—to pivot or to persevere—take courage, but I

would argue that the choice to persevere takes more, due to our culture's dismissiveness regarding the reality of trade-offs, our fear of failure, and the analysis paralysis that creeps in when you have too many options. In the words of the author of *The Paradox of Choice*, "Learning to choose is hard. Learning to choose well is harder. And learning to choose well in a world of unlimited possibilities is harder still."[18] If you believe you have found your one thing and you are on the cusp of choosing to persevere on the path to mastering it, let these three truths give you the courage to take the leap.

First, remember that there is no "right" decision. Just like finding a spouse, there is no Mr. Right, but there is a Mr. Best in discerning your calling. Choosing your vocation is not about choosing between good and bad or right and wrong. It is about choosing between better and best. It is about examining your options and making a deliberate decision to choose the work that best combines your passions and gifts in an attempt to declare the excellencies of God and love your neighbor as yourself through masterful work.

> **Choosing your vocation is not about choosing between good and bad or right and wrong. It is about choosing between better and best.**

Second, if you are on the brink of choosing your one thing, be encouraged by the fact that there are few irreversible decisions. Making the choice to persevere in your pursuit of mastering one thing today doesn't mean that you can't pivot to something better two, ten, or twenty years down the road. In all my interviews for this book, not a single master said that they knew how long they would spend focused on their one thing. There's just no way of predicting how the Lord will move in your life and career. You aren't necessarily choosing to commit to something for the rest of your life. You are choosing the best opportunity to do the most exceptional work in this season of life.

Finally, remember that if you desire to do your most excellent work and make the greatest contribution to the world, there is an imperative to make a decision and commit to a path to master. I am a huge fan of Lin-Manuel Miranda, the musical theater genius behind *Hamilton, In the Heights,* and *Moana.* At the height of the popular mania surrounding *Hamilton, 60 Minutes* ran a profile on the musical and Miranda's path to mastering the art of musical theater. When asked how he achieved such monumental success in his field, Miranda reflected back to his days in school, saying, "You know, I went to a school where everyone was smarter than me. And I'm not blowin' smoke . . . I was surrounded by genius, genius kids. What's interesting about growing up in a culture like that is you go, 'All right, I gotta figure out what my thing is. Because I'm not smarter than these kids. I'm not funnier than half of them, so I better figure out what it is I wanna do and work really hard at that.'" The *60 Minutes* interviewer pressed Miranda further, asking, "So why do you think I'm sitting here talking to you and not sitting here talking to one of your classmates?" Miranda replied, "'Cause I picked a lane [musical theater] and I started running ahead of everybody else. So . . . that's the honest answer. I was like, 'All right THIS.'"[19]

For reasons we have already explored, choosing one thing to pour all of our professional energies into is essential to doing our most excellent work. Not everyone is given the gift of finding their one thing. If the Lord is gracious enough to reveal where your passions and gifts can intersect with an opportunity to do your best work for his glory and the good of others, it is your responsibility to steward that revelation by committing to that work and working at it with all your heart. We shouldn't settle for doing mediocre work if we discover a vocation the Lord has clearly equipped and called us to do with mastery. It is our responsibility to make the most of the gifts and time the Lord has given us so that one day, we might hear him say, "Well done, good and faithful servant" (Matthew 25:23).

In his letter to the Philippians, the apostle Paul wrote, "And this I pray, that your love may abound still more and more in real knowledge and all discernment, so that you may approve the things that are excellent, in order to be sincere and blameless until the day of Christ" (Philippians 1:9–10, NASB). Expounding upon this passage, former Moody Bible Institute professor J. Hampton Keathley III once wrote:

> The pursuit of excellence is never a matter of simply choosing between what is good or bad, but of choosing what is best or superior because it will better enable us to accomplish what God has designed us to be and do. In keeping with the fact that all believers are to abound or excel in the expression of Christian love, the apostle prayed that the Philippians [may] have greater knowledge and every kind of discernment. But in order to excel in love and wisely express it, they needed to be able "to approve the things that are excellent" (NASB) or choose what is best. . . . Through the values and priorities that come from the knowledge of God's Word, we are to examine and test, and then choose accordingly.[20]

Once you have taken the time to "examine and test" your hypotheses about what your one thing might be, it is critical that you come to a point at which you choose the one thing you will do most exceptionally well for the glory of God and the good of the world.

In July 2004, the one thing Scott Harrison cared about most was getting out of New York City. For years Harrison had built a career as one of the city's most successful nightclub promoters, throwing parties with A-list celebrities including Jay-Z, Heidi Klum, and Sean Penn. But after reading a copy of A.W. Tozer's *The Pursuit of God*, Harrison "declared spiritual, moral, and emotional bankruptcy" and was slowly looking for a path to exiting his "boozy" lifestyle.[21] But one day a nightclub bouncer named Eddie forced Harrison to expedite his timeline for leaving the city. At a club early one morning, Eddie had infuriated Harrison, causing him to wield his power to call the bouncer's boss to get him fired. The next day Eddie showed up at Harrison's home with a gun. Not finding Harrison there, Eddie hopped around town, looking for Harrison at his favorite clubs. That's when Harrison got a call from a friend who had just run into the furious ex-bouncer. "Scott, he's really pissed," the friend told Harrison. "He said he wants to kill you." Looking back on the incident, Harrison said, "I couldn't believe it. This guy was hunting me."[22]

The incident was enough to, quite literally, run Harrison out of town and end his career as a club promoter. Once out of New York City, Harrison composed himself and started to explore what he might do next. Understandably, he wanted to get as far away from New York City as possible, so he decided to volunteer a year of his life as a photojournalist for Mercy Ships, a fleet of floating hospitals that offer free lifesaving surgeries for people where medical care is nearly nonexistent. Harrison boarded a ship to Liberia and breathed a sigh of relief that he was beginning to leave his former life in New York behind.

Once in Liberia, Harrison was exposed to the most gut-wrenching, abject poverty imaginable. It didn't take long for God to radically transform Harrison's heart. The man who once referred to himself as "Lord

Scott Harrison" was now beginning to yearn for a life modeled after the Lord Jesus Christ, spent in service of "the least of these." The question for Harrison was where he would even begin to make a dent in serving the world's poorest people. While onboard his Mercy Ships vessel, Harrison would frequently seek out counsel from Dr. Gary Parker, the chief surgeon for Mercy Ships, whose initial three-month stint of volunteering his valuable surgical skills had turned into a thirty-year commitment to the cause. In one of their frequent chats onboard the ship, Harrison confided in Dr. Gary, saying, "I really want to help the poor, but there's just *so* much need. We're sending patients back to homes that have no roofs. Children are going back to villages with no schools. It's all so overwhelming. I don't even know where to begin."[23]

Harrison didn't know exactly how he could best serve the poor, but by the time his stint with Mercy Ships was up, he had made up his mind that he would be moving back to New York City to start a charity of his own. Forever transformed by the Holy Spirit and his experience in Liberia, the former club promoter was truly a "new creation." Soon after his arrival stateside, Harrison opened a bank account and deposited every penny he had ($1,100) to start his new charity. "Now I just had to figure out what this new charity would actually do," Harrison said. To help gain clarity on that question, Harrison shot an email to Dr. Gary, writing, "I'm starting my own charity. . . . Should I focus on access to surgeries, malaria nets, health clinics, education, justice, shelter, water?"[24]

As Harrison recalled, "I think he could tell that my head was spinning with ideas. I wanted to do it all. Thankfully, Dr. Gary provided a much-needed voice of reason: 'Scott, rather than five or ten different issues, perhaps God wants you to focus on one intensely,' he counseled. 'Pick that one issue carefully.'"[25]

Just *one* thing. The idea was so simple and appealing to Harrison who had witnessed firsthand the tremendous impact Dr. Gary had made by committing his life to helping solve a single humanitarian problem. Harrison was sold, but now he had to do the hard work of discerning what his one thing would be. As he explored many options, Harrison thought back to a conversation he had at a bar in Liberia with some humanitarian doctors who were familiar with the diseases that were causing the need for so many surgeries aboard Mercy Ships. "All these diseases are largely preventable," one of the doctors shared. "Most of them would just go away with good water and sanitation. And *then* you could focus on the other crucial issues around poverty." At first, Harrison thought this was unbelievable. But it didn't take long for him to independently confirm what the doctors had told him. "The more I learned, the more I realized those doctors weren't exaggerating when they said that dirty water and lack of sanitation caused half of all illnesses in the developing world. The real number was 52 percent. For years, dirty water was the number one cause of disease and death worldwide. It killed more people than all the wars, terrorism, and violence in the world combined."[26]

Harrison had found one cause worth choosing to commit to, so he gave his nascent nonprofit a name and a mission—charity: water would exist to bring clean and safe drinking water to people in developing countries. Harrison's laser-like focus on this one cause has allowed charity: water to make a truly incredible impact, providing clean water to more than eight million people around the world thus far.[27]

There's no way Scott Harrison could ever have had this type of impact without emphatically saying yes to his one thing—providing clean water to every person on the planet. But equally important is what he chose to say no to—raising money for education, shelter, medical care, or economic development. As we have explored in this chapter, the path to mastery is full of left/right decisions. But once you've said yes to your one thing and chosen to persevere down a particular path, it is equally important to say no to everything else that falls outside your chosen path to mastery. It is that process of elimination that we now turn to in the next chapter.

Chapter Summary

In order to do your most exceptional work for God's glory and the good of others, it is essential that you choose to "go big" on one vocational thing. Choosing to commit to one thing is hard given our tendency to want to "do it all." But if you think you've found your one thing and you are looking for the courage to commit, remember these truths: (1) There is no right or wrong decision. (2) There are few irreversible decisions. (3) If you seek to do your best work for God's glory and the good of others, there is an imperative to make a decision.

Key Scripture

"Whatever you do, work at it with all your heart, as working for the Lord, not for human masters" (Colossians 3:23).

Next Action

If you are ready to choose your one vocational thing, take the time to write it down to memorialize your commitment. I have created space for you to do this in the "Master of One Notebook," which you can download for free at jordanraynor.com/MOO.

Chapter 7

Eliminate

Only once you give yourself permission to stop trying to do it all, to stop saying yes to everyone, can you make your highest contribution towards the things that really matter.

GREG MCKEOWN

One year after choosing to commit to a career as a full-time designer, Emily Ley (whom you first met in chapter 5) was overwhelmed trying to build her business, care for her newborn, and keep up with all the other commitments she had made in her life. As she explained, "I took client calls while nursing. I worked frantically during nap times. And playtime at the park was a regular event for the three of us— me, [my son, Brady], and my iPhone. Instead of enjoying the best parts of a job I loved and a child I adored, I burned my candle at both ends trying to keep up."

But Ley wasn't keeping up and she knew it. Then one day the perfect storm of circumstances converged, forcing her to concede that something had to change. As Ley recalls, "One morning, I paced a circle around my house attempting to multitask. I can still remember the sound my bare feet made on the laminate wood floor while I bounced three-month-old Brady in the carrier strapped to my stomach. I was helplessly trying to pacify him and answer a design client's questions about the breakdown of her new brand colors. I tried to sound peppy and focused so the client knew I was devoting all my attention to her, but Brady was clearly ready to be fed. After the call was over, a flood of tears and frustration washed over me."

At the end of her rope, Ley called a friend and said, "I'm failing at everything. Everything. . . . I thought I could do it all. I thought I could be the picture-perfect mom running the picture-perfect business, but

I'm just so tired. I haven't washed my hair in days. I'm failing everyone. I've got to find a new standard."[1]

Ley's new standard started with recognizing what was essential in her life and eliminating everything else that wasn't. Ley was clearly saying yes to mastering one thing professionally—building her design business—and she was also committed to being an excellent mother and wife. But there were many other things she chose to say no to, both professionally and personally. For example, Ley has said no to always having the Pinterest-perfect house and cooking gourmet meals every night for her family, knowing that there is simply no way to do this all well while also mastering the building of her growing design business and being an excellent wife and mother. "We eat a lot of takeout and pizza on the floor," Ley explains, "and it totally works for us. . . . I give myself grace and permission to not be Supermom in the kitchen. . . . Pizza on the floor on Fridays is delicious and fun and totally okay. Paper plates, napkins, and delivery from our favorite local spot . . . means happy kids, full bellies, and not-stressed-out Mom and Dad."[2]

More recently Ley made the decision to eliminate her wholesale business, which allowed her to quickly place her planners in more than eight hundred retail stores globally. While this was a very profitable line of business, Ley was overwhelmed and didn't feel as if she had the bandwidth to master her role as wife and mother, her wholesale business, and the entirely separate line of business that she was most passionate about: selling her planners directly to consumers via her website. Many people would scratch their heads at the decision to turn off such a significant wholesale business. But Ley understands that in order to make her greatest contribution toward the few things she is choosing to say yes to, she has to get really good at eliminating the nonessential from her life.

The list of things Ley is pursuing excellence at is small, but she pours everything she has into those things. This has allowed her to maintain a healthy marriage and relationship with her kids while also building a global brand that's impacting the lives of hundreds of thousands of other busy women. "I [used to be] determined to prove to the world that I could do it all," Ley shared. "But by the grace of God, I realized this critical truth: that even if you can do it all, no one can do it all *well*. . . . The only way to lighten an overfull plate is to take things off it—to quit things, to say no, to uncommit."[3]

Intuitively, I think we all understand Ley's words to be true. We all want "less but better" in our lives, yet our natural instincts are to say yes to nearly every opportunity that comes our way. There are many reasons why *no* is such a difficult word to utter on a consistent basis, but for the Christian, it appears particularly difficult due to a misplaced sense of service. When we are clear on the work we are choosing to master, we feel a sense of guilt saying no to good things, even though we know they will distract us from our path to mastery. So we agree to serve on yet another committee at church, take on a nonessential project at work, and begrudgingly agree to "just grab coffee" with someone looking to "pick our brains," even though we know that precious time could be better spent serving others by pursuing mastery of our one thing. We fear that by saying no we are being "bad Christians" who are selfishly unwilling to serve those around us. Nothing could be

> **If we are unwilling to say no to the nonessential in order to focus on the work we feel called to master, we are selfishly holding back the contribution God has called us to make in the world.**

further from the truth. Ironically, what on the surface may look like selflessness is actually quite selfish. As pastor Timothy Keller said:

> Of course there are many of us who *look* unselfish and dutiful, simply because we can't say no: We say yes to everything, and people are always using us. Everybody says, "Oh, you're so selfless, so giving of yourself; you need to think more about taking care of yourself." But think about those of us who don't have boundaries and who let people walk all over us and use us and can't say no—do you think we're doing that out of love for other people? Of course not, we're doing it out of *need*—we say yes to everything out of fear and cowardice. That's far from glorifying others.[4]

If we are unwilling to say no to the nonessential in order to focus on the work we feel called to master, we are selfishly holding back the contribution God has called us to make in the world. Nobody understood this principle better than Jesus who worked with a staggering amount of focus as he pursued the work the Father gave him to do (see John 17:4). One of the first scenes of Jesus's ministry illustrates this well:

> As soon as [Jesus and his disciples] left the synagogue, they went with James and John to the home of Simon and Andrew. Simon's mother-in-law was in bed with a fever, and they immediately told Jesus about her. So he went to her, took her hand and helped her up. The fever left her and she began to wait on them.
>   That evening after sunset the people brought to Jesus all

the sick and demon-possessed. The whole town gathered at the door, and Jesus healed many who had various diseases. He also drove out many demons, but he would not let the demons speak because they knew who he was.

Very early in the morning, while it was still dark, Jesus got up, left the house and went off to a solitary place, where he prayed. Simon and his companions went to look for him, and when they found him, they exclaimed: "Everyone is looking for you!"

Jesus replied, "Let us go somewhere else—to the nearby villages—so I can preach there also. That is why I have come." (Mark 1:29–38)

As Mark opens up his account of Jesus's ministry, he shows the Savior on a healing spree, driving out demons from a man in the synagogue, healing Peter's mother-in-law, and healing "many" from the "whole town" who showed up at Jesus's door. Not surprisingly, the next morning the disciples rushed to Jesus and said, "Everyone is looking for you!" Obviously, the town had gotten wind of Jesus's miraculous powers to heal and wanted an encore on day two. But in what must have come as a shock to the disciples, Jesus said no and offered an alternate itinerary: "Let us go somewhere else . . . so I can preach there also. That is why I have come."

This is the first, but certainly not the last time we hear Jesus say no in the Gospels, so it's worth stopping to ask why he refused to serve more people through his miraculous powers of healing. Clearly, he had the power to heal more people. He undoubtedly had the desire to alleviate the pain in these people's lives. But while Jesus may have wanted to heal more people, he knew he had limited time on earth to fulfill his purpose. Jesus didn't come to earth just to heal and reveal his identity.

He came to preach the gospel in preparation for the Passion he would perform on the cross. Jesus was crystal clear regarding his purpose—his one thing—and this led him to consistently say no to good things in order to focus on the essential work the Father gave him to do during his time on earth.

This resoluteness became increasingly clear as his ministry neared the cross. As we've already seen, in Luke 9:51 we are told, "When the days drew near for [Jesus] to be taken up, he *set his face* to go to Jerusalem" (ESV, emphasis added). I *love* that phrase. Jesus knew his purpose. He knew exactly what he was saying yes to. But this clarity wasn't enough. Once he understood his mission, Jesus had to resolutely "set his face" in focused pursuit of his most essential work, saying no to the many nonessential things along the way.

If Jesus couldn't say yes to everything, neither can we. Our time to live out our calling is limited. As we saw in the previous chapter, this is why it is so important that we choose the one thing we believe God has called and equipped us to do most exceptionally well for his glory and the good of others. And once that choice has been made and we are heading further down the path to mastery, it is critical that we, like Jesus, "set our face" in focused pursuit of mastering our one thing, constantly saying no to opportunities—even really good ones—that distract us from the essential work the Father has given us to do.

Remember John Mark Comer, the pastor you met in chapter 1 who realized early in life that he was never going to be a basketball star? One of the things I respect most about Comer is his laser-like focus on the work God has called him to and how this clarity helps him say no to the long list of other things vying for his attention. On this topic Comer is worth quoting at some length. Here's what he said:

I'm called to lead my church, teach the Scriptures, and bring my family along for the ride. That's what I'm saying *yes* to, which means, I have to say *no* all the time.

I'm a pastor, and so . . . people want me to . . . have something TED-talk quality to chat about for forty minutes *every* Sunday, meet with fifty people every week for coffee, keep the staff healthy, . . . go through a thousand books a year, pop on social media a few times a day, write a blog, pump out a book every so often, have the picture-perfect marriage and family . . . —oh, and stay "healthy."

Now, that's all great stuff. Superpastor would kill it at that job. But I'm not superpastor. I'm John Mark. Obviously I can't do all that in one lifetime.

So I'm constantly saying *no*. . . .

To borrow from the language of Jesus, you gotta figure what the "work the Father gave you to do" is.

And then you need to learn the art of saying no. . . . Because when you get sucked into the tyranny of the urgent . . . you put off what's really important. When you say *yes* to *everything,* you say *yes* to *nothing.* The work the Father gave you to do gets put on the back burner, at the bottom of the to-do pile. This is a tragedy because you're robbing the world of your much-needed contribution.[5]

It's not just Jesus's example and the words of wise Christian leaders like Comer that call for us to get in the habit of saying no. Today's best business literature is chock-full of similar wisdom. Peter Drucker, likely the most influential management thinker of the twentieth century, said, "People are effective because they say 'no.'"[6] In his book *Great at Work*, Morten Hansen (coauthor of Jim Collins's classic *Great by Choice*) found that this principle, which he calls "do less, then obsess," is the number one predictor of how effective someone will be in a particular job. I particularly like how Ryan Holiday, best-selling author of *The Obstacle Is the Way* and *Ego Is the Enemy*, talks about the need to eliminate the nonessential in order to pursue mastery of our chosen one thing:

> There are many different missions. Whatever yours is, it must be defined and articulated.
>
> Once that has occurred, there is one last thing you must do. You must deliberately forsake all other missions. . . . If you've committed to doing something incredibly difficult that countless others have failed at before, you probably also shouldn't be juggling five other projects at the same time. You'll need to put 100 percent of your resources toward this one.
>
> Nothing has sunk more creators and caused more unhappiness than this: our inherently human tendency to pursue a strategy aimed at accomplishing one goal while *simultaneously* expecting to achieve other goals entirely unrelated.[7]

In other words, once you've chosen the one thing you are going to pursue mastery at professionally, it is critical that you get really good at eliminating things that promise to distract you from your essential mission.*

---

* In the "Master of One Notebook" you will find prompts to help you identify nonessential activities you may want to say no to in order to better focus on mastering your one thing. To download the free notebook, visit jordanraynor.com/MOO.

THE PROCESS OF ELIMINATION

While getting in the habit of saying no takes discipline and hard work, the process isn't rocket science. In fact it's quite simple. Here's an example of how I have seen the process of elimination play out in my own life.

Say Yes to the Essential

Following the example of Jesus, before you can decide what to eliminate from your life, you need to be crystal clear on what is essential. Professionally, this is the one thing you have chosen to master in this season of life. A few years back I was running a thriving consulting business helping entrepreneurs grow their businesses. One of my most promising clients was Threshold 360, whose founders were on an audacious mission to allow anyone to virtually step inside any location on earth. A year into my consulting engagement with the company, the founders asked if I would consider taking over the reins as the startup's second CEO. While the move required a ton of sacrifice and risk, I couldn't pass up the opportunity. I was (and continue to be) ecstatic about the mission of Threshold. I also knew I wasn't going to make my greatest contribution to the business as a part-time consultant. I needed to put all my eggs in that basket. So I did. I gave an emphatic yes to applying my one thing (entrepreneurship) to just two projects: bringing Threshold 360 to market and launching the book I had just finished writing (*Called to Create*).

But my work wasn't the only thing I was choosing to deem essential in my life. As we explored in chapter 1, we Christians are called to excellence in everything we commit ourselves to. So while I had chosen to sink my teeth into Threshold sixty hours a week, I also had a few things other than work that I was committed to pursuing with excellence: my marriage, raising my kids, a handful of friendships, and being an active participant in the life of my home church. The list of things I was saying yes to at this stage of my life was quite short, but each item takes an extraordinary amount of time and energy to pursue with excellence. This unavoidable truth caused me to make a much longer list of things I was intentionally saying no to in order to focus on what was truly essential.

Say No to the Nonessential

Once you've chosen your one vocational thing and identified what's essential outside of your work, it is critical that you get good at saying no to the nonessential in order to pursue excellence at the things that really matter to you. When I decided to commit to the role of CEO at Threshold, I had to say no to a lucrative consulting practice and the clients I loved. I also chose to eliminate many activities that took me away from my wife and kids at night, knowing that, in my new role, I was going to be traveling much more than before. This meant saying no to some really good things, including serving on the boards of a few organizations, playing piano at my church on Wednesday nights, and even a couple of Bible studies. But the biggest sacrifices by far were made by my wife, Kara.

My wife is brilliant. And that's not just a proud husband talking. I've got data to prove it. After graduating with a crazy-high GPA from Florida State University, Kara earned her master's in accounting and sat for the Unified Certified Public Accountant (CPA) Examination, widely regarded as one of the most difficult professional exams. It's so difficult, in fact, that fewer than 10 percent of exam takers pass all four parts of the test in their first sitting.[8] Kara is one of the 10 percent.

After receiving her CPA license, Kara started a stellar career in finance, climbing the corporate ladders at Ernst & Young and Raymond James Financial. But when we decided that I would take the leap and join Threshold full time, Kara made the choice to walk away from her career, at least temporarily. We both knew what my new role demanded: much more stress, much less flexibility, and significantly more time on the road. Given our commitment to being exceptional parents, there was simply no way I could be an excellent CEO of the venture if Kara was pursuing mastery of her financial services career at the same time. Something had to give. And Kara graciously and sacrificially chose to put her career on hold so that I could focus on pursuing mastery in mine. We've seen plenty of people excel as mothers and fathers while also pursuing mastery at their respective vocations. But we knew our personal limits and agreed we couldn't both be chasing our ambitious professional dreams *and* give our kids the attention they needed. Even though the sacrifice was huge, Kara chose to put her career on hold to focus on her role as a mother—the one thing she felt she was called to pursue with mastery at that stage in her life.

Beware of Side Paths

Kara and I live in a coffee desert. The closest Starbucks is five miles away, and the closest local coffee shop is even further. Every few months I get the urge to invest in opening a café near our house. Without fail Kara graciously listens to my ridiculous quarterly pitch: "Babe, this is a no-brainer opportunity. It will be easy. We can even get so-and-so to run it. It's not that big of a lift. We won't have to lift a finger after six months!" After my entrepreneurial rant is over, Kara just stares at me. She knows better, and she knows I know better. No entrepreneurial activity is ever "small," even if you aren't managing the operation day to day. Our "coffee shop conversation" always ends the same way, with Kara reminding me that while this would be a fun project that is in line with the one thing I have chosen to master (entrepreneurship), in this particular season of life, there is simply no way either of us can take on another major project and do it exceptionally well.

Here's my point. The process of elimination is not just something you do one time. As you continue down the path to mastery, there will be many side paths vying for your attention, attempting to distract you from the work the Father has given you to do. In these moments it is important to remind yourself of what is essential and have someone alongside you to keep you focused on the path to mastery. For me, that's usually Kara or my closest friends. For Chip Gaines, it was a Twitter follower.

———

Chip Gaines and his wife, Joanna, are the founders of Magnolia Homes and Magnolia Market, a home goods store that takes up two city blocks in Waco, Texas. But those businesses aren't what catapulted the Gaineses to becoming household names. That came when HGTV asked the couple to star in their own reality TV show, *Fixer Upper,* based on the couple's construction and interior design business.

One sleepless night before a day of filming the show, Chip picked up his phone, opened Twitter, and read, "Hey @chippergaines it's been 3 weeks, and I still haven't gotten my wreath. What's up?!"

As Gaines shared, "I wasn't happy about that [tweet], of course. But I tried to shake it off, knowing that I couldn't do anything about it then and that it would have to wait until morning. No luck. I was up all night dwelling on it. And Jo and I were scheduled to film . . . the next morning, hair combed, by eight o'clock."[9]

Something about that tweet struck a nerve with Gaines, so much so that it caused a significant distraction on set the next day. As he explained, "Midway through our second shot of the day, I started to get this weird, not-good, fuzzy feeling. I thought I must just be exhausted or dehydrated or something like that. I found a place to sit down and let my mind settle. But as I was sitting there, all of a sudden I was overwhelmed by a single thought. *What am I doing here?*"[10]

Gaines was experiencing the pain of realizing he had traveled pretty far down a side path that was causing him to lose focus on mastering his one vocational thing—the couple's business. Part of the reason the Gaineses agreed to do the TV show in the first place was for the free advertising it would generate for Magnolia Homes and Magnolia Market. But once the show launched, its popularity skyrocketed, as did the demands on the couple's time. Now instead of having two massive priorities in their life, they had three: their family, their business, and their show.

"Against our better judgment, we told ourselves that 'We've got it'—that we could, in fact, keep juggling our three priorities. That they weren't actually that big," Gaines said. "But guess what? We didn't actually have it. It was really easy for us to feel like we could do it all when the show and the business were in the early stages. But the bigger things got—and they got big *fast*—the less energy we had to devote to all three. So much time was being allocated to filming that the details of the business were slipping. But it was easy for us to fall into the illusion that the business was doing just fine with a third of our attention."[11]

It took a tweet to get a sleepless Gaines to realize he couldn't do it all and that the TV show had become a side path distracting him from the work he and Joanna felt called to master. That's when the Gaineses shocked the world by announcing that they would be walking away from *Fixer Upper* at the height of the show's massive success.

It's one thing to say you believe the principles of this book. It's another to put your money where your mouth is when there is *a lot* of money on the line. But that's exactly what the Gaineses did. "We've never had more at stake. This decision may severely affect our finances as well as our opportunities," Chip explained. "It almost seems nonsensical to walk away from this miraculous gift from God. . . . I feel a bit like the biblical patriarch Abraham standing at his makeshift altar, arms around his precious son, facing the enormous sacrifice he believes he is being called to make. *The Lord gives and the Lord takes away, and in all these things we're to bless him!* Obviously, leaving a television show behind is not in the same stratosphere as sacrificing one's son, and I'm certainly no Abraham. And yet I feel as though Joanna and I have gotten a small taste of that struggle. We have wrestled every which way with this decision, and still we end up on the same side: It's time for us to lay it down."[12]

Through this experience the Gaineses have gained greater clarity on their purpose and their limits as parents and business owners. As Chip explained, "While we Gaineses may be workhorses, we're also pretty clear on what our limitations are. Joanna and I have concluded that we can only do two things *really* well at one time," and one of those things is raising their family. "It's not that we can't juggle more than two things at a time," Gaines said. "We just don't do it well. Something's eventually gotta give."[13]

With significant wealth and sizable teams to help them run their ventures, it's safe to say that Chip and Joanna Gaines have more resources than most of us reading this book. And even with all those assets, the Gaineses have admitted they can't do more than one thing masterfully well at a time vocationally. Coming to this decision one time isn't easy, but sticking with it is even harder. Just a year after admitting they can't do two vocational things really well at the same time, the Gaineses announced that they would be returning to TV, this time with their own cable network. Will the couple find a way to ensure that TV more closely aligns with their one thing—the couple's work as entrepreneurs? Or will TV continue to be a side path distracting the Gaineses from the work they feel called to master? Only time will tell.

There's a reason why most people don't achieve mastery at their chosen craft: the path to mastery is hard—*really* hard—fraught with difficult decisions to continually eliminate good things in order to focus on the one thing you believe the Lord has called you to do. But it is only when we make those brave decisions to say no to distracting side paths that we are able to continue down the path to mastering the one thing we are enthusiastically saying yes to.

Chapter Summary

Once you have chosen the one thing you will master vocationally, it is of paramount importance that you eliminate as much as you can from your professional plate in order to focus on doing your very best work. If you are unable to say no to the nonessential in order to focus on your one thing, you will be holding back the contribution God has called you to make in the world.

Key Scripture

"When the days drew near for [Jesus] to be taken up, he set his face to go to Jerusalem" (Luke 9:51, ESV).

Next Action

Give yourself permission to say no to the nonessential in your life so that you can focus on what you're saying yes to personally and professionally. Make a list of projects, commitments, or relationships you will eliminate in order to focus on mastering your one thing.

Chapter 8

Master

Lots of people want to be the noun
without doing the verb.

AUSTIN KLEON

Once you've chosen your one thing and eliminated all other distractions, how do you become masterful at your vocation, ensuring you are doing your most excellent work for the glory of God and the good of others? Throughout my extensive research and interviews for this book, the same answers to that question came up over and over again. Those answers—what I believe to be the three keys to mastery—are the subject of this final chapter of part 2. The three keys to mastery are submitting ourselves to the teaching of other masters through apprenticeships, purposeful practice, and discipline over time. Let's now closely examine each of these three keys.

KEY #1: APPRENTICESHIPS

In James 4:6, we are told that "God opposes the proud but shows favor to the humble." The Lord's faithfulness to this promise shone through vividly in my research for this book. More than any other quality, humility marked the stories of every Christ-following master I spoke with. While it's clear that humility is a key character trait throughout the entire path to mastery, it is of particular importance immediately upon choosing the one vocational thing you will master. Once we have found the work we are going to sink our teeth into, it is of the utmost importance that we humble ourselves and seek out the mentorship of others who are already masters in our chosen field. In my research for this book, there was near unanimous consensus across business literature and my interviews that the most common path to mastery includes some form of apprenticeship.

Apprenticeship isn't a word you hear a lot these days, but the practice is something you see time and time again in the world's most masterful people. Now, there are two types of apprenticeships: direct apprenticeships and indirect apprenticeships. A direct apprenticeship is what you likely have in mind when you first hear the word *apprentice,* defined as "a person who works for another in order to learn a trade."[1]

> **Humility is a key character trait throughout the entire path to mastery.**

This concept may sound foreign, like something only fifteenth-century artists and carpenters did when access to information and social networks was severely limited. But the practice of direct apprenticeships is very much alive today. In fact, nearly all the masters whose stories fill this book entered into a direct apprentice relationship once they chose their one thing: David Boudia entered into a direct apprenticeship with his diving coach. Jeff Heck apprenticed under far more experienced financiers at his private equity firm before taking the reins at Monday Night Brewing. And Fred Rogers apprenticed at NBC and under the tutelage of the world's leading child psychologists before creating *Mister Rogers' Neighborhood.*

The second form of apprenticeship is the indirect apprenticeship in which you humbly submit yourself to the wisdom of masters but do so without personal relationships with or direct feedback from them. This is similar to the self-taught model of learning new skills. Emily Ley is a good example of this. At the start of her career as a graphic designer, Ley humbly admitted she didn't know what she was doing and "googled a million questions and watched all the YouTube tutorials" she could get her hands on.[2] That indirect apprenticeship with virtual masters put Ley on her own path to mastery, leading to the tremendous growth of her design business.

Whether you choose a direct or indirect apprenticeship, the key is to humbly submit to the teachings of masters with far more experience and expertise in your chosen one thing. This posture of humility can be quite countercultural. In his book *Mastery,* Robert Greene explains why:

> We live in a culture that likes to criticize and debunk any form of authority, to point out the weaknesses of those in power. If we feel any aura, it is in the presence of celebrities and their seductive personalities. Some of this skeptical spirit toward authority is healthy, particularly in relation to politics, but when it comes to learning and the Apprenticeship Phase, it presents a problem.
>
> To learn requires a sense of humility. We must admit that there are people out there who know our field much more deeply than we do. Their superiority is not a function of natural talent or privilege, but rather of time and experience. Their authority in the field is not based on politics or trickery. It is very real.[3]

Greene goes on to concur with what many other students of mastery have independently concluded: while indirect apprenticeships can lead to mastery, by far the most common path to mastering any skill is through a direct apprenticeship with a mentor who has already mastered your chosen one thing. This aligns with what I found in my interviews for this book. Of the dozens of masters I studied, less than a handful achieved mastery without a direct apprenticeship. While both direct and indirect apprenticeships can offer tremendous value, the direct route is—by nature of the word—the most efficient path to mastery. As

Greene explained, "The mentor-protégé relationship is the most efficient and productive form of learning. The right mentors know where to focus your attention and how to challenge you. Their knowledge and experience become yours. They provide immediate and realistic feedback on your work, so you can improve more rapidly."[4]

I've found these words to be true not only by studying the lives of the masters in this book but also in examining my own personal experience pursuing mastery as an entrepreneur. Early in my career I didn't have a formal mentor. Instead I spent my time in indirect apprenticeships, reading every book I could about the work of great entrepreneurs such as Walt Disney, Marissa Mayer, and Jeff Bezos. But I have never had a direct relationship with Bezos, Mayer, or Disney, and more importantly, I have never had the opportunity to work with these great entrepreneurs so they could really get to know me, spot my unique challenges, and coach me through overcoming those obstacles. While I continue to grow as an entrepreneur by studying the lives of masters like these from a distance, the growth I have experienced from those indirect apprenticeships is much less than what I have experienced in direct apprenticeships.

There are many good reasons to take on investors in a venture. But in my experience the very best reason is that, with the right investors, you are buying access to a direct apprenticeship with a mentor who is financially invested in your success. During my time as CEO of Threshold 360, I had the distinct honor of working alongside some incredible investors who are phenomenally successful entrepreneurs in their own right. Because these investors had a financial interest in my team's success, they were "in the trenches" with me, available whenever I had a question or was struggling with a big decision in leading the venture. They also helped me spot weaknesses in myself and my team and worked with me to improve those underdeveloped areas of the business. This process of direct feedback wasn't something that happened sporadically. On a very regular basis, I had the ability to access our investors for direct, specific feedback. In the few years I spent running Threshold day to day, I learned exponentially more than during the entire rest of my ten-year career as an entrepreneur. In other words, while I continued to grow as an entrepreneur through indirect apprenticeships during this time period, it was my direct apprenticeships that allowed me to travel exponentially faster down the path to mastery.

While direct apprenticeships are preferable as you seek to master your one thing, not everyone is blessed with access to the right mentor. Oftentimes we gain access to the right mentors through connections and social capital. In the case of Fred Rogers, his direct apprenticeships came through the relationships of his wealthy parents. Rogers's family was a major stockholder in the Radio Corporation of America (RCA), which in the 1950s owned NBC. This allowed Rogers's father to call in a favor to help secure an apprenticeship at NBC for his son, Fred.[5]

You certainly don't need to come from a wealthy family in order to find the right mentor, but the truth is there are many factors that make it difficult to secure direct apprenticeships. In the case of Emily Ley, it wasn't necessarily a lack of social capital that led her to choose an indirect apprenticeship over a direct one. It was a lack of time. There was simply no way Ley could have entered into an intense, apprentice-like relationship with a master designer while she kept her day job and cared for a toddler at home. If you are struggling to find the right direct mentor to help you master your one thing, an indirect apprenticeship may be your best option at this point on your path to mastery. As many masters like Ley have learned, indirect apprenticeships can indeed be valuable means of honing the skills you are seeking to master. If you are considering an indirect apprenticeship, here are three tips to make this process as valuable as possible.

First, don't think of yourself as being "self-taught," think of yourself as an "apprentice." What may seem like semantics can actually have a big impact on your mind-set—putting you in the right frame of mind to learn and grow with humility.

Second, be selective when choosing the masters to study under in an indirect apprenticeship. We are living in a time of unprecedented amounts of information and advice. In this flood of content, it can be difficult to discern the true masters from the posers. Take the time to carefully consider whose mentorship you will submit yourself to virtually and then, once you've made your choice, go all in and devour everything they have to say.

Finally, if you have chosen an indirect apprenticeship, lean in to the advice of those virtual mentors, but be sure to stay on the lookout for a direct apprenticeship that's right for you. Again, while indirect apprenticeships can be quite valuable, you are almost guaranteed to learn exponentially faster in a direct apprentice/mentor relationship.

Scott Harrison learned this lesson firsthand. After leaving the nightclub scene to start a charity to bring clean water to the world, Harrison realized he knew very little about how to run a nonprofit. So he humbly submitted himself to the authority of the *Nonprofit Kit for Dummies*. But as Harrison experienced, indirect apprenticeships like the ones you get from books can only take you so far. While *Dummies* gave Harrison a lot of information (for example, what the word *bylaws* means for a nonprofit), the book didn't know Harrison personally and thus couldn't coach him through the specific steps he had to take in order to become the leader charity: water needed him to be.

"I always thought of charity: water as a startup. And yet, I'd never even worked in a real office before," Harrison said. "I had no clue what a startup was actually like, much less what a CEO was supposed to do all day."[6] Harrison knew that in order to master his role as CEO of charity: water, he needed to enter into a direct apprenticeship with an entrepreneur who had been successful in a similar position.

That's when Harrison was introduced to Ross Garber, an incredibly successful tech entrepreneur who grew a company from zero to three hundred fifty employees in three years and an eventual valuation of more than $15 billion. Clearly, Harrison had a lot to learn from someone like Garber about how to run and scale an organization. "I told him I really needed a mentor," Harrison shared.[7] Thankfully, Garber agreed, and the two made plans to kick off the direct apprenticeship by spending a few days together in New York where Garber could observe Harrison's management style up close and personal at charity: water's offices.

Once on site Harrison launched into a speech about his lofty vision for charity: water: "I want to raise $2 billion for clean water by 2020," he told his new mentor.[8] Garber listened and then looked around the office to find an immature organization being led by an inexperienced leader. On his flight back home, Garber wrote a scathing eleven-page memo to his new protégé. As Harrison recalled in his book *Thirst*:

He called my "$2 billion by 2020" vision "statistically impossible" and "ridiculous," and listed my blind spots as a leader.

"Charity: water is a shop of fifteen people, but a team of exactly one. You," Ross wrote. "You control everything. You even run everything. You are the product design guy. The merchandising guy. The fundraising guy. The message guy. Probably even the check-signing guy. . . . Metaphorically, if you're still in the club biz, you can either be the bartender or running the show. . . . You can't mix the drinks and run the whole club."

Ross said I needed to start thinking like a CEO, which meant grow up, stop worrying about day-to-day details, and start focusing on big-picture, multi-year goals.

"Whether history records you as a success or failure," Ross warned, "will depend on whether you can shift from living in today to living in tomorrow."

It was some of the best advice I'd ever gotten.[9]

Garber continued to mentor Harrison for four years after that first meeting, and the two spoke by phone constantly and emailed each other dozens of times a day. "His replies were sometimes brutal," Harrison wrote, "ripping into me for dumb things I'd said ('You're totally undisciplined!') or done ('Stop demanding that everyone read your mind!'), or written to my employees ('Scott, don't send them wet noodle, do-nothing notes like this')."[10]

Unlike an indirect apprenticeship with a book or YouTube videos, Harrison's direct apprenticeship allowed an expert to spot his unique strengths and challenges and coach him to rapidly master the art of building an amazing organization. "[Garber] taught me how to zero in, reframe priorities, and get out of my own way," Harrison shared.[11]

Today, charity: water is one of the world's leading nonprofits, and Harrison credits Garber for playing a huge role in that success. But Harrison deserves a lot of credit as well. Most people don't humble themselves in the way Harrison did, readily admitting they don't know everything and subjecting themselves to harsh but valuable feedback. One of charity: water's core values is that they "love feedback, even when it hurts."[12] There's no doubt that much of Garber's feedback was painful for his apprentice to hear, but the humility to listen to it and apply it was critical to Harrison's development into a master leader in his own right.

KEY #2: PURPOSEFUL PRACTICE

If you've read any business book in the past ten years, you are probably familiar with The Ten-Thousand-Hour Rule, as it is likely the best-known insight on the science of mastery, etched into business folklore by Malcolm Gladwell in his bestseller *Outliers*. In the book Gladwell cites an academic paper published by Dr. Anders Ericsson, who has been called "the world's leading expert on experts,"[13] in which Ericsson and his team of researchers sought to understand what leads to master-ful performance. Is it natural talent as conventional wisdom suggests? Practice? Or something else entirely?

To put these questions to the test, Ericsson and his team studied the practice habits of a group of violin students throughout childhood, adolescence, and adulthood. All the students had begun playing the violin around the age of five with similar amounts of practice times dedicated to their instrument. But by the age of eight, the amount of time the violinists spent practicing began to diverge significantly. By the time the students turned twenty years old, the most elite violinists had averaged more than ten thousand hours of practice each, while the less able performers had averaged just four thousand hours of total prac-tice.[14] The study concluded that "many characteristics once believed to reflect innate talent are actually the result of intense practice" over a long period of time.[15] Citing Ericsson's findings, Gladwell went on to coin The Ten-Thousand-Hour Rule, saying that "Ten thousand hours is the magic number of greatness."[16]

There's a lot to love about Gladwell's rule, not least of which is its elegant simplicity. There's just one problem. According to Ericsson— the scientist behind the study Gladwell based his rule on—Gladwell grossly misinterpreted the original study and oversimplified the far more complex science of mastery. While Ericsson affirms that it is practice and not "natural talent" that is the best predictor of exceptional performance, he has sharply criticized Gladwell for failing to make the critical distinction that it's not just any sort of practice that leads to extraordinary work. It is only what Ericsson refers to as "purposeful practice" over long periods of time that leads to mastery. In other words, the secret to the violinists' success was not just in how much they practiced but, more importantly, in *how* they practiced for those ten thousand hours.[17] And it is in this principle of purposeful practice that we find the second key to mastery.

So, what distinguishes "purposeful practice" from mere practice, or what Ericsson calls "naive practice"? Naive practice is "essentially just doing something repeatedly, and expecting that the repetition alone will improve one's performance."[18] Purposeful practice, as the term suggests, is much more deliberate and intentional. In his book *Peak: Secrets from the New Science of Expertise,* Ericsson outlines four elements of purposeful practice that we must understand and apply in order to achieve mastery of our one thing.

Specific Goals

First, purposeful practice requires that you have specific goals that you are aiming toward. Let's say you have chosen to make writing your one thing. It's not enough to say, "I want to be an excellent writer" and spend hours every day hammering away at your laptop, churning out content. That is not purposeful. In order for your practice as a writer to be purposeful, you need to turn your amorphous objective ("I want to be an excellent writer") into a specific goal ("I want to sign a book deal with one of the five largest publishers").

Once that more specific goal is well defined, it is important to break down your larger objective into smaller, more narrowly defined goals. For example, maybe you struggle with writing attention-grabbing first sentences that plunge readers into your chapters or blog posts. In this case, purposeful practice might include reading the first couple of sentences of your favorite authors' works, studying what makes them effective, and aiming to write three dynamite opening lines of your own. According to Angela Duckworth, the author of *Grit* and another expert on the study of mastery, purposeful practice includes "zeroing in on just one narrow aspect of . . . overall performance" and working deliberately to improve that particular skill.[19] Then, once that skill is mastered, you can build on it, bringing you closer and closer to mastery and achieving your larger goals. In the words of Ericsson, purposeful practice is "all about putting a bunch of baby steps together to reach a longer-term goal."[20] But unless those goals are specific and well defined, your practice will be naive and your work less than masterful.

Intense Focus

The second element of purposeful practice is the ability to intensely focus on the specific goals you have established. In Ericsson's study of violinists, the most elite performers didn't just practice more than their counterparts. When they practiced, they did so with an intense focus, typically working in three or four ninety-minute blocks of totally focused, uninterrupted practice time each day. Once specific goals are defined, masters embrace this type of deep work, eliminating distractions in order to focus intensely on the task at hand.

Of all the elements of purposeful practice, this is the one I am most passionate about personally, as I believe the practice of deep work is the single most important practice in my day-to-day pursuit of mastery. If you were to look at my calendar, you would see that I break my day into four ninety-minute blocks of deep work, with time for short breaks, email, and meetings (shallow work) interspersed throughout the day.* Once I am "in a block," I am laser focused on accomplishing the specific goal in front of me. My office door is closed. My noise-canceling headphones are on. My phone is on Do Not Disturb. And the only things open on my laptop are Spotify, OmniFocus (my task-management system), and whatever tool I am using to accomplish my specific goal in that block (usually a Google Doc).

Throughout my interviews for this book, the theme of intense focus arose time and time again. David Boudia puts his headphones on to eliminate distractions before a big dive at the Olympics. Jessica Jones stays intensely focused when she is caring for newborns in the NICU. Josh Eicholtz's focus during his preflight checklist could make the difference between life and death in Papua New Guinea. Once specific goals are set, masters set themselves apart by intensely focusing on the task at hand.

Rapid Feedback

The third element of purposeful practice is rapidly receiving feedback on how you have done in pursuit of your specific goals. As Proverbs 12:15 says, "The way of a fool is right in his own eyes, but a wise man listens to advice" (ESV). People who are mediocre at their work don't feel the need to seek advice from others; but those on the path to mastery

---

* I've included a sample of my daily calendar in the "Master of One Notebook," which you can download for free at jordanraynor.com/MOO.

earnestly seek out feedback. I like the way Duckworth describes this process in *Grit*: "As soon as possible, experts hungrily seek feedback on how they did. Necessarily, much of that feedback is negative. This means that experts are more interested in what they did *wrong*—so they can fix it—than what they did *right*."[21]

As we've already explored, getting feedback on your work from mentors is important, but it's equally important to get feedback from those you serve. After all, for the Christian, the purpose of mastery is glorifying God and loving others as ourselves. It is simply impossible to know if we are loving and serving others well through our work if we aren't seeking their feedback. If you are a writer, get feedback from your readers. If you are an entrepreneur, get feedback from your customers. If you are in client service, get feedback from your clients.

My friend Mike Allen is a great example of this element of purposeful practice. Described by the *New York Times Magazine* as "the man the White House wakes up to," Allen's morning email summarizing the political news of the day is the most sought-out piece of journalism inside the Beltway, read religiously by nearly every political junkie in Washington. Mike, a devout follower of Jesus Christ and one of the most humble people I know, views his work as service to the world, and that leads him to earnestly seek out feedback from everyone: mentors, colleagues, and readers alike. Allen takes the principle of rapid feedback so seriously that he personally reads and responds to every piece of feedback he receives from readers via email, whether it's from the White House chief of staff or an intern on Capitol Hill.

Frequent Discomfort

According to Ericsson, "Perhaps the most important part of purposeful practice" is "getting out of one's comfort zone," and never feeling as if you have arrived.[22] Once a specific skill has been mastered to the point at which it has become routine, masters raise the bar, forcing themselves to move outside their comfort zone to continue to push the envelope of what's possible in their craft. As Duckworth explained, "Rather than focus on what they already do well, experts strive to improve specific weaknesses. They intentionally seek out challenges they can't yet meet."[23]

At Threshold 360 one of our core values is being "humble, scrappy, and hungry." Here's how we describe the core value to new hires: "We are executing a massive vision, and when a new milestone is reached or a new problem is solved, it can be tempting to believe 'we have arrived.' We haven't. There's always another threshold, and that keeps us humble, scrappy, and hungry to make the most of the opportunity we have been given." Masters think the same way about their chosen crafts.

As I interviewed Jeff Heck, the CEO of Monday Night Brewing, he sat in his office under a flag that reads "better is possible." I can think of no more succinct way to summarize this last element of purposeful practice. Mastery requires a belief that "better is possible," constantly pushing past the comfort of what has already been achieved, always looking to become more and more masterful at our one thing.

KEY #3: DISCIPLINE OVER TIME

Once we have chosen the one thing we will master vocationally, we must first humble ourselves and submit to the authority of experts in our field. Second, we must learn how to practice our craft in a purposeful, deliberate way. Finally, we must work at mastering our craft with incredible discipline over long periods of time.

There are two types of discipline exhibited by masters that set them apart from their less masterful counterparts. First, they exhibit daily disciplines and routines. C. S. Lewis is a great example of this. According to his stepson Douglas Gresham, Lewis followed the same disciplined routine nearly every day (waking up at four or five in the morning, spending time in prayer and God's Word, making himself breakfast, responding to letters, and then focusing intensely on his current writing project). Almost all the masters interviewed for this book have daily disciplines like these that help them make steady progress toward their goals. But there's a second type of discipline that sets these masters apart, and that is the discipline to stay committed to one thing over a long period of time: Lewis spent nearly thirty years mastering his role as a teacher at Magdalen College. David Boudia put in more than ten thousand hours of purposeful practice before winning Olympic gold. Christy Adams has spent nearly fifteen years honing her skills as an educator.

As we've seen in this chapter, the science is indisputable: To become truly masterful at any vocation, you must have the discipline to spend thousands and thousands of hours purposefully practicing that one thing. This is why it is so important to take the proper time to explore many different career opportunities before choosing to commit to your one thing. Because it's not enough to make a choice. In order to do our most masterful work, we must find one thing worth staying committed to over a significant period of time.

That takes a level of commitment that is uncommon today. "Enthusiasm is common. Endurance is rare," according to Angela Duckworth, likely the most highly regarded expert on the science of perseverance.[24] Summarizing her personal experience and years of research on the topic of mastery and grit, Duckworth said that "repeatedly swapping out one career ambition for another is unfulfilling" and that while "being a 'promising beginner' is fun . . . being an actual expert is infinitely more gratifying."[25]

Why? Because passion follows mastery. As we have seen throughout this book, it is when we get insanely good at something that we love and serve our neighbors well through our work and in doing so find the deep satisfaction of vocation and passion for our work that is sustainable over a long period of time. But achieving that level of mastery takes discipline and time—*lots* of time. In a world full of quick fixes and get-rich-quick schemes, that truth can be a difficult pill to swallow. But it is truth. Indisputable, undeniable truth. As Scripture reminds us time and time again, nothing but "diligent hands will rule" (Proverbs 12:24). In the words of Duckworth, "There are no shortcuts to excellence. Developing real expertise, figuring out really hard problems, it all takes time—longer than most people imagine. . . . Grit is about working on something you care about so much that you're willing to stay loyal to it. . . . It's doing what you love, but not just falling in love—*staying* in love."[26]

If we are going to do our most exceptional work for God's glory and the good of others, we are going to need to commit to "staying in love" with one thing vocationally and put in the disciplined effort it takes to become masterful at the work the Father has given us to do. We are going to need a tremendous amount of passion, discipline, and grit. In the words of Jeff Heck and the team at Monday Night Brewing, we are going to have to "fight for excellence."

I love the way Heck and his team describe this core value of the brewery: "We never settle for 'good enough,' because we understand the virtue of patience in order to win the fight." When I asked Heck why he and his cofounders describe the pursuit of excellence as a "fight," he said, "Because inertia pushes us toward mediocrity. Excellence is something you have to be proactive about. If you want to do something excellent, it requires a tremendous amount of time, energy, and effort. You have to fight for it."[27]

Heck and the masters throughout this book understand that, in order to do our most masterful work for the glory of God and the good of others, we must be humble, purposeful, and disciplined, intentionally fighting for something more excellent than we achieved the day before. Excellence does not come naturally. Almost everything in this world pushes us toward quick fixes, shortcuts, and "good enough." But the exceptional, Christ-following professionals in this book show us that there is a better, more disciplined, more excellent, more God-honoring way. Choosing that path— the path to mastery—requires that we "press on toward the goal" (Philippians 3:14) of pouring our best selves out as an offering to God and others. It requires that we fight for excellence, always striving to become more masterful at our chosen work.

> **Choosing the path to mastery requires that we fight for excellence, always striving to become more masterful at our chosen work.**

As we come to the end of part 2 of this book, I feel it's time to share something a kinder author might have shared at the beginning of the journey: There is no end to the path of mastery. Mastery is not a destination but a lifelong journey of continually honing our crafts in order to more effectively declare the excellencies of our Creator and serve those around us, always believing that "better is possible." As we've seen in this chapter, mastery requires humility, purposeful practice, and tremendous discipline and perseverance over time. Mastery isn't something that is granted to us, it is something we have to fight for. The question then becomes, "Is the fight really worth it?" That's the question we will answer in the final part of this book as we look at the tremendous promises of masterful work.

―――――――

Chapter Summary

There are three keys to mastering your one thing. The first is a direct or indirect apprenticeship. The second is what scientists call "purposeful practice," which distinguishes itself from "naive practice" in that it requires specific goals, intense focus, rapid feedback, and frequent discomfort. The third and final key to mastery is having the discipline to stick with your one thing over a long enough period of time to become truly masterful at it.

Key Scripture

"Diligent hands will rule, but laziness ends in forced labor" (Proverbs 12:24).

Next Action

Write down the element of purposeful practice that you need to develop most, along with specific actions you will take to make this a part of your regular work process.

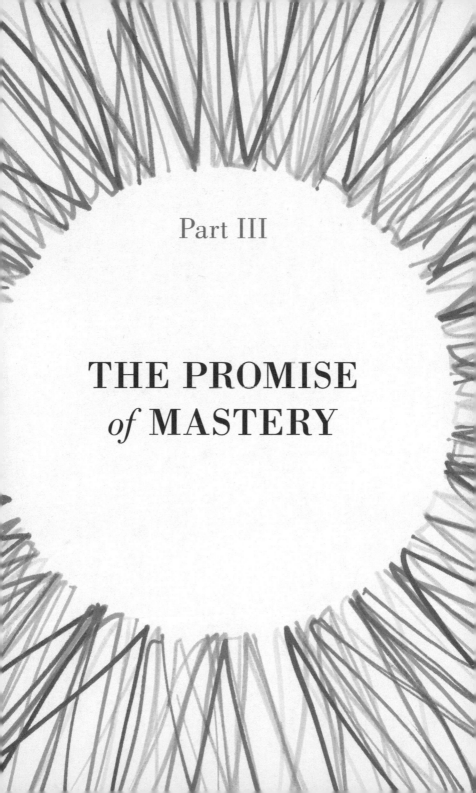

Part III

THE PROMISE
of MASTERY

Chapter 9

Salt and Light

No matter the sport, no matter the human endeavor really, total effort will win people's hearts.

PHIL KNIGHT

In part 1 of this book, we saw that the most fundamental purpose of mastery in our work is to glorify God and love our neighbors as ourselves. As if that wasn't enough to spur us on in our fight for excellence, the Lord has graciously offered up a number of promises that provide us with extra motivation as we pursue mastery in our work. It is those promises we now turn to in this third and final part of the book. But before we dig into the first promise of mastery, we need to take a quick trip to Hollywood to study the burgeoning world of "Christian entertainment."

It seems like every few months, churches across the United States are promoting a new overtly evangelical movie. From a purely financial standpoint, the boom of the "Christian film industry" makes a lot of sense, as these films can be *crazy* profitable. But while the economic impact of these movies is significant, their cultural impact is nearly nonexistent. It's no secret that entertainment made by the church and for the church is seen by virtually nobody outside the church. As Andy Crouch pointed out, "Any cultural good . . . only moves the horizons for the particular public who experience it. For the rest of the world, it is as if that piece of culture . . . never existed."[1]

Why is it that these films are only relevant within the church? Why aren't these movies winning the respect of Christians and non-Christians alike? It's because the undoubtedly well-intentioned filmmakers behind these movies seem more interested in pushing their agenda than the boundaries of their art form. They focus almost exclusively on the message of their films rather than on mastery of their craft. This, it turns out, is a recipe for producing mediocre work that fails to earn the respect of the world.

Two-time Academy Award winner Andrew Stanton knows a thing or two about excellence in entertainment, with credits that include *Finding Nemo, Toy Story,* and *Stranger Things.* Stanton is also a follower of Christ, but one who is careful not to prioritize pushing his personal agenda over becoming more and more masterful at the art form the Lord has called him to pursue. "My personal view is that if you go into things on a pulpit or with an agenda in the creative world, it can easily get in the way of your creativity and quality,"[2] Stanton said. Hip-hop artist Lecrae, another masterful Christian culture creator, put it more bluntly, "Christians have really used and almost in some senses prostituted art in order to give answers instead of telling great stories and raising great questions."[3]

As Stanton and Lecrae point out, when personal agendas take precedence over being true to the work the Lord has called us to master, it leads to mediocrity, not mastery. While mediocre, agenda-first products may win the respect of a small subset of people desperate for products that preach their values, they fail to win the respect of those outside the church. But when we focus first on producing exceptional work, our work will inevitably earn the respect of Christians and non-Christians alike, thus making us and the God we serve winsome or, at the very least, credible. This is the promise of mastery. Pastor Timothy Keller summarizes this idea well:

> Cultural change is always a by-product, not the main goal.
> The main goal is always *loving service.* If we love and serve
> our neighbors, city, and Lord, it will definitely mean social

changes, but Christians must not seek to take over and control society as an end in itself. If we truly seek to serve, we will be gladly given a certain measure of influence by those around us. If we seek power directly, just to get power and make the world more like us, we will neither have influence nor be of service.[4]

Lecrae is a great example of how this truth plays out in the music industry. He is the first artist to ever land an album at the top of both the Billboard 200 and the gospel charts simultaneously, and his work is respected by those inside and outside the church. How has he pulled this off? By prioritizing mastery of his craft over the message of his music. "In the same way that Jesus was a carpenter, I don't know if he put his message into all the things he built with his hands," Lecrae said. "I think he wanted to make good quality craftsmanship." Lecrae seeks to follow the model of his Savior in how he crafts his music. And while you certainly see evidence of Lecrae's faith in his songs (in one track he raps about "the sole redeemer"), it is clear that pushing a particular message is secondary to being the most masterful artist he knows how to be. As the author of an article in the *Atlantic* wrote, "Perhaps that's why Lecrae has built unprecedented popularity across genres: He's not trying to preach—he's just trying to do his art."[5]

In Hollywood, *The Passion of the Christ* and *The Chronicles of Narnia: The Lion, the Witch, and the Wardrobe*, as well as NBC's *This Is Us* provide further examples of how exceptional work makes Christian values attractive to the world. Each of these cultural goods contains deeply Christian themes and storylines, yet they are all wildly popular pieces of media, viewed by millions of Christians and non-Christians alike. Why? Because they are first and foremost masterful movies and TV shows. Their creators made something worth seeing and sharing. These films and shows are true to their art forms, and because of that, they and their underlying messages win the respect and affections of the world.

C. S. Lewis was one of the most influential culture creators of the twentieth century. According to his stepson Douglas Gresham, Lewis used to say, "We do not need more people writing Christian books. What we need is more Christians writing good books."[6] This belief led Lewis to prioritize becoming a master teacher through the medium of literature rather than pushing any particular message or agenda through his books. Speaking about *The Lion, the Witch, and the Wardrobe* specifically, Gresham said that, contrary to popular belief, "[Lewis] never set out to write anything in the way of a Christian story. When he was a child, he read lots of books by good children's authors. And when he looked around at what was being issued to children in his own adult life, in the 1950s, he found that as far as he was concerned most of it was garbage. So, he thought it would be a good idea to try to write a children's story of the sort that he himself would have loved to have read as a child. When he started on the work, the Holy Spirit of God took over, and that's why they turned into the books they did. But, at the onset of *The Chronicles of Narnia*, it wasn't [Lewis's] intention to preach. His intention was to simply write a really good book."[7]

Today, Gresham carries on his stepfather's legacy as a masterful culture creator in his own right, as the producer of Disney's hit *Chronicles of Narnia* films along with other Lewis-inspired projects. It's clear that Lewis's view of how masterful work wins the respect of the world rubbed off on Gresham. "I don't think movies should be used as a preaching element," Gresham said. "For a Christian in any art form or any business or any work in the world, the most important thing of all is to do the work right and to do it well. That's what Christianity is all about. Doing the right thing and doing it well."[8]

Gresham, Lewis, Lecrae, and Stanton are all hitting on the same truth: one of the greatest promises of mastery is that when we do our work exceptionally well—focusing first and foremost on serving others rather than pushing a particular agenda—we win the respect of the world and earn the right for our message to be heard. In other words, we fulfill Jesus's call to be the "salt of the earth" and the "light of the world." In the Sermon on the Mount, Jesus used these two peculiar word pictures to describe his church, saying:

> You are the salt of the earth. But if the salt loses its saltiness, how can it be made salty again? It is no longer good for anything, except to be thrown out and trampled underfoot.
>
> You are the light of the world. A town built on a hill cannot be hidden. Neither do people light a lamp and put it under a bowl. Instead they put it on its stand, and it gives light to everyone in the house. In the same way, let your light shine before others, that they may see your good deeds and glorify your Father in heaven. (Matthew 5:13–16)

When Jesus said we are to be the salt of the earth, he called us to be winsome and attractive to those around us. Jesus calls us, as Christians, to bring flavor to life—to be the kind of people others naturally want to be around. When we do that, much like salt, our lives cause others to thirst for what is true and different in our lives. In other words, our "saltiness" gives us opportunities to reflect the Light of the World, namely Christ.

While Jesus has called us to be salt and light in every aspect of life, there is perhaps no more powerful and practical way to fulfill this call than in our chosen work. The tent-making apostle Paul understood this, which is precisely why he instructed us to "work with your hands, just as we told you, so that your daily life may win the respect of outsiders" (1 Thessalonians 4:11–12). But as we've seen, not all work "wins the

> **When we do our work exceptionally well—focusing first and foremost on serving others rather than pushing a particular agenda—we win the respect of the world and earn the right for our message to be heard.**

respect" of the world. Mediocrity is appealing to no one. But when you and I do our work with mastery, we will win the respect of outsiders and become the salt of the earth Jesus has called us to be, making the world thirst for him. But what does it look like practically for masterful work to pay off in this incredible way? To answer that question, we'll look at the stories of a banker, a coach, and an entrepreneur on a mission to end homelessness.

Soon after we got married, Kara and I joined a Bible study led by Wade Griffin. It didn't take long for me to recognize that Griffin was a master of his craft, having spent thirty years in banking, most recently as the national head of checking and debit sales for Bank of America. Now, I know virtually nothing about the world of finance and banking (a fact that my CPA wife can attest to), but Griffin's high-profile role alone instantly won my respect. As a young professional I wanted to soak up as much career wisdom as I could from Griffin, and in a short time, he became one of my closest mentors. Over the years I've learned that I'm not the only one whose respect Griffin has won by being a master of his craft. For decades, Griffin's mastery of his profession has allowed him to be salt in his community, winsome and inspiring to nearly everyone he comes in contact with.

When I sat down with Griffin nearly ten years after our friendship began, I asked him what motivated him to set such high standards of excellence in his work as a banker. His response caught me off guard, taking me all the way back to his days as a child working alongside his grandfather on a farm in the hot and humid South. "My grandfather was one of the biggest influences in my life," Griffin told me. "This was a guy with a fourth or fifth grade education, and while he was not super affluent, he did quite well for himself given his upbringing. He was just an incredibly hard worker. And, as a kid, I absolutely *loved* spending time with him and working with him on the farm. I can still remember being with him in the middle of summer, in the middle of the day in south Georgia, sitting on the hood of his tractor with my feet dangling on the headlights as we plowed up and down the fields. There was no place I'd rather be. Even though I was sitting on top of a hot motor in the hot sun, I just wanted to be with him."

Griffin's grandfather taught him a valuable lesson: masterful work wins the respect of others and makes us the salt of the earth—the kind of people that others naturally want to be around in ways that are some-times difficult to put into words. That lesson left an indelible mark on Griffin as he started his own career. After college, while he was search-ing for his first job, Griffin was also searching Scripture for a verse that he could embrace as a theme for his life. "Fairly early on in my career, I was really seeking clarity within my faith. I wanted to know what spe-cifically the Lord wanted my life to be about," Griffin shared. "I grew up kind of a country boy. I hadn't traveled much. I was not well read. But because of the example of my grandfather and others in my life, I was always attracted to performance. I was attracted to good things—not for the sake of flashy, expensive toys and cars necessarily. But I was definitely attracted to contributing."

That desire for performance, productivity, and contributing to the world through his work led Griffin to choose Colossians 3:23 as the verse he would build his life around: "Whatever you do, work heartily, as for the Lord and not for men" (ESV). Griffin shared, "That verse just became ingrained in me, and so I really began to apply that in every area of my life, including my work." Remembering the example of his grandfather, Griffin knew that if he did his work "heartily," or masterfully well, he would honor the Lord, win the respect of others, and be the salt of the earth Jesus calls us all to be.

That promise proved to be true from early on in Griffin's career, as he quickly won the respect of his bosses, causing him to rise rapidly through the ranks at Barnett Bank, the largest commercial bank in Florida at the time. As Griffin focused on serving his employer well, he was rewarded with promotion after promotion and raise after raise. But it wasn't just the respect of his bosses that Griffin won. Throughout his career, Griffin's excellence won him the highest respect of his colleagues and employees.

As we were sitting in his office, Griffin was reminded of some "very kind comments" his employees shared with him as he was leaving a leadership role at a Barnett location in Jacksonville. Griffin walked over to his bookshelf to find the comments, and while I was expecting him to come back to our interview with a flimsy Hallmark card in hand, he handed me a large leather-bound book filled with notes from his former team. One note in particular stood out to me. Griffin's former employee wrote, "You and one other are the only bosses I would work for again. I don't know how you did it, but you piqued my interest with regards to Jesus."

By prioritizing serving his employer and employees masterfully well over pushing any personal agenda, Griffin won the respect of others. He became credible to those around him. In large part due to Griffin's example, at least one of his employees surrendered his life to Christ. While Griffin was clearly grateful that the Lord allowed him to be used in this powerful way, he was quick to point out to me that his agenda as a banking executive was never exclusively or even primarily to make disciples at the office. His priority was to be the most masterful banker he could be, glorifying God and serving his employer and employees well in the process. That is precisely what won the respect of outsiders. As Griffin explained in retrospect, "I've heard stories of people who got fired from their jobs for sharing the gospel at their office, and I always thought, *Oh my word, that's terrible! You're stealing time that you're being paid by your employer to push your personal agenda.* That's just not honoring to the Lord Jesus Christ. I was always very mindful of that. At the office I was an employee first. I was being paid to do a job, and I wanted to do that job masterfully well. I wasn't shy about my faith, but I wanted to live out the gospel first. And I always felt like the most effective gospel presentation I can ever give is when somebody came to me and said, 'There's something different about you.' If you have to go tell people how different you are from them, then you probably aren't all that different."⁹

When we focus on getting masterfully good at our one thing, we win the respect of the world. We become the salt of the earth that makes others thirsty to be around us and long to understand what makes us tick. And this gives us unparalleled opportunities to shine the light of Christ to the world.

Almost nothing wins the respect of the world more than victory at the highest level of sports. Leading up to Super Bowl XLI, this thought was at the forefront of Tony Dungy's mind. "I knew that if we won, they would bring me up to the podium, ask me a couple of questions, and I would have forty-five seconds to speak to 120 million people," Dungy shared with me.[10] But Dungy didn't allow himself to "put the cart before the horse" and write the speech before the big game. It wasn't until Dungy glanced up at the scoreboard to see that his Colts were up by twelve points with just two minutes left in the game that he started to sketch out the speech in his head.

"I can remember that moment very vividly," Dungy told me. "I remember as the clock ticked past the two-minute mark, I was thinking about my mom and dad, and elementary school coaches and teachers, and everybody that poured into my life. I was just very thankful and grateful." Then the clock passed the one-minute mark and Dungy thought, "Okay, now I *really* have to figure out what I am going to say. What do I want these 120 million people to know?"[11]

Dungy knew that this victory would earn him more respect and attention than he had ever experienced before. And he wanted to be sure that the millions of people watching the game understood what motivated him to work with such a high standard of excellence. So when the interviewer asked Dungy how it felt to be the first African American coach to win the Super Bowl, Dungy said, "I tell you what, I'm proud . . . to be the first African American to win this. It means an awful lot to our country. But . . . more than anything, [I'm proud to be a Christian coach] showing that you can win doing it the Lord's way."[12]

As Dungy and I talked about that speech more than a decade later, he explained that "I wanted the world to see that you can follow the Lord's principles and still win and still be excellent and get to the top. I wanted to direct people to that. That was my motivation for winning. In our world today, we love excellence, we love winners. So, when you are excellent at something, you are going to be attractive to people and you can redirect that attention to Christ."[13]

Dungy hit the nail on the head. Mastery in our work—be it making a movie, running a bank, or coaching a team—makes us attractive to the world. Then, once we have been graced with the world's attention, we have the privilege and responsibility of being signposts pointing to Jesus Christ. For Dungy, that meant proclaiming the name of Jesus to more than one hundred million people watching the Super Bowl. For most of us, being the light of the world will look quite different. But regardless of how high profile our one vocational thing might be, the Lord can use our mastery of our craft to create opportunities to make disciples of Jesus Christ—a promise Brett Hagler can personally attest to.

On a cool March day in Austin, Texas, hordes of entrepreneurs, designers, developers, and technophiles are swarming the city's convention center for SXSW, the annual convention that draws tens of thousands attendees, each hoping to catch a glimpse of the next great innovation.[14] Not far from the convention center, twenty-seven-year-old Brett Hagler stands watching his team's technical innovation come to life as a robot lays thick concrete in perfectly straight lines. The sight of the massive machine stops SXSW conference-goers in their tracks. As a crowd of interested observers begins to gather, they quickly realize that this is unlike any other 3-D printing project they've seen before. Hagler and his team aren't printing cheap plastic iPhone cases or drink coasters. They're printing a home!

In less than twenty-four hours, the project is complete—Hagler and his team have become the first to use a 3-D printer to build a home that is fully up to code and complete with a certificate of occupancy. Reporting on this triumph of ingenuity, one media outlet said, "In the near future, building a new home may be as easy as printing out an airline boarding pass." The fact that the technology exists to print a livable eight-hundred-square-foot home in less than a day is mind blowing; but what's even more incredible is the cost to build the house. This first-of-its-kind prototype cost just $10,000 to build, and Hagler is confident that he and his team can bring that cost down to just $4,000 per home.[15]

What I find most interesting about Hagler's innovation is that, rather than using it to extract healthy profits out of the tiny house movement, he is bringing this incredible technology to serve "the least of these" first. The next homes will be printed in El Salvador, providing safe shelter to some of the country's poorest residents for the very first time. This is just one of many initiatives Hagler is leading under New Story, the nonprofit he cofounded with the ambitious, gospel-fueled mission to end homelessness by providing safe shelter to the more than one billion people globally who are without adequate housing.

Fueled by his faith and the example of Jesus Christ, Hagler is pouring his life out sacrificially to solve one of the biggest humanitarian problems of our time. But this Brett Hagler is a relatively new creation—a radically different person from the kid who spent his college years chasing fame, fortune, glory, and girls. As Hagler explained, "During those years, I didn't really care about helping other people. I cared about one thing: optimizing my personal fulfillment and happiness, which I thought came from things like being more popular, having higher status, the prettiest girls, traveling around the world, and ultimately being 'the man' compared to everybody else."

Much like the prodigal son, Hagler was running away from the Christian values he grew up with. "I went to a Christian school. I grew up in the church. But I was not a good church boy. I wasn't a believer. I had serious objections to this whole Christian thing," Hagler shared. When I asked Hagler what the source of those objections was, he said, "I just thought Christians were boring. I thought the church was too judgmental. And there just weren't enough people, in my opinion, who had big goals or were striving for excellence with their lives."

Ambitious from an early age, Hagler looked around his Christian community and couldn't find compelling examples of Christians who were masters of their crafts. To him (and so many others), this made the church far from appealing. In the words of Jesus, the salt had lost its saltiness. "I was kind of like, ehh, that's really not for me," Hagler said. "That really turned me off to Christianity."

So what led to Hagler's radical life change? "It started shortly after college when I was raising money for my first startup," he explained. "And I met this investor who I grew to really respect. He just had a really high level of excellence. He was a master of his craft. And I just thought he was a cool guy. I could relate to him. He was somebody that, in my dreams, I would love to be like one day. I just wanted to be around this guy and soak up as much professional wisdom as I could."

What Hagler didn't know at the time was that this investor was a Christian. But unlike the Christians Hagler knew growing up, this gentleman was earning Hagler's respect, and he was doing it by being a world-class master of his vocation. "I had no clue he was a believer,"

Hagler shared, "and then one day, I was asking him some questions about leadership, and in a really cool and casual way, he started to share his philosophy of leadership with me. And it was modeled after Jesus. So, this guy that I have grown to respect professionally is sitting there, explaining that the reason why he is who he is, is because of his faith and because he follows Christ. Given my upbringing and what I thought Christians looked like out in the marketplace, that just really blew me away."

> **When you and I pursue mastery of our chosen work, we fulfill our call to be the salt of the earth.**

Soon after that conversation Hagler surrendered his life to Jesus Christ and began pursuing mastery of his craft not as a means of accumulating fame and fortune, but as a means of glorifying God, serving others, and making disciples of Jesus Christ. Hagler—who was once pushed away from the Christian faith because of a perceived lack of excellence in the lives and careers of Christ followers—was drawn back to Christianity in large part because of one man's mastery of his vocation. "God used that man to just totally destroy all the wrong thoughts I had about Christianity," Hagler said. "This was somebody I really wanted to be like professionally. That's what drew me in. And then, once he had my respect and my attention, I was just very open to hearing the gospel in a fresh new light."[16]

As we've seen in this chapter, when you and I pursue mastery of our chosen work, we fulfill our call to be the salt of the earth. We become winsome to the world, causing others to want to learn more about what drives us in our pursuit of excellence. Once we have earned the world's attention, the Lord graciously creates opportunities for us to share the gospel and make disciples as we seek to glorify him through our masterful work. What a tremendous promise! What an incredible responsibility.

―――――――――

Chapter Summary

While the most fundamental purpose of mastery in our work is to glorify God and love our neighbors as ourselves, the Lord has graciously offered up a number of promises that provide us with extra motivation as we pursue mastery of our one thing. The first promise is that when we do our work masterfully well—focusing first and foremost on serving others, rather than pushing a particular agenda—we win the respect of the world and become the salt of the earth, making the world thirst to learn more about the Light of the World.

Key Scripture

"Let your light shine before others, that they may see your good deeds and glorify your Father in heaven" (Matthew 5:16).

Next Action

Make a list of people you've been drawn to in the past because of their commitment to excellent work. Take a minute to allow that list to inspire you to pursue mastery as a means of being salt and light to those you work with.

Chapter 10

The Room Where It Happens

When I was a boy I used to think that strong
meant having big muscles, great physical
power; but the longer I live, the more I realize
that real strength has much more to do with
what is not seen. Real strength has to do with
helping others.

Fred Rogers

It's two o'clock in the morning, and Sherron Watkins is wide awake. While her husband and two-year-old daughter sleep soundly in their cozy Houston home, Watkins is lying in bed, silently rehearsing what she will say in tomorrow's all-important meeting. On the other side of the desk at this appointment will be Ken Lay, founder and chairman of Enron, where Watkins is employed as a vice president. On this night—August 21, 2001—Enron is still a darling of Wall Street, worth more than $60 billion. But in less than four months, the company will be bankrupt, in large part due to the conversation Watkins is planning as she tries to catch some sleep.

Not long before this sleepless night, Watkins, an accountant turned high-ranking executive at Enron, had uncovered what appeared to be fraudulent accounting practices at Enron. Her first attempt to sound the alarm bells within the organization was to write an anonymous memo to Lay ahead of a company-wide meeting that would include time committed to addressing anonymous questions submitted by employees. Watkins didn't mince words in her memo, saying, "I am incredibly nervous that we will implode in a wave of accounting scandals."[1]

But when Lay didn't address Watkins's concerns directly at the all-hands meeting, she knew she had to come out of the shadows and put her name and face to the memo outlining her concerns about the company. That's when Watkins secured thirty minutes on Lay's calendar to sound the alarm directly, risking her career in the process. That meeting was one of a few sparks that set off a massive cover-up and the rapid collapse of the once mighty Enron. After the firm filed for bankruptcy on December 2, 2001, federal regulators would corroborate Watkins's findings, exposing the widespread fraud to the world and leading to the conviction of Lay and the imprisonment of many Enron executives.

While Watkins was ultimately unable to save the company or stop thousands of employees from losing their jobs and retirement savings, the Lord still used her in a powerful way to put an end to the sinful fraud Enron had been engaged in on an unprecedented scale. And because of her willingness to leverage her position of power sacrificially in service of others, Watkins was recognized by the United States Congress and the American people for her bravery and courage. She was even named *Time* magazine's Person of the Year in 2002 along with two other whistleblowers who made headlines that same year. As the *Time* article reported, "These women . . . did right just by doing their jobs rightly—which means ferociously, with eyes open and with the bravery the rest of us always hope we have and may never know if we do. Their lives may not have been at stake, but [they] put pretty much everything else on the line. Their jobs, their health, their privacy, their sanity—they risked all of them to bring us badly needed word of trouble inside crucial institutions."[2]

It's clear that Watkins did a difficult but God-honoring thing in blowing the whistle on Enron, but what's also clear is that Watkins would likely have never been in a position to do so had she not been a master of her craft. For starters, she needed to be masterful at the skills of accounting to spot the fraud that so many others missed or kept quiet about. But she also needed to be masterful at her one thing in order to attain a position of power that allowed her to catch the attention of Enron's chairman. Due to her seniority in the firm and her previous presentations to the company's board of directors, Watkins knew Lay—

not well, but well enough to secure a meeting on his calendar, a seemingly impossible feat in a company with nearly thirty thousand employees. If she had been an entry-level accountant at Enron, it's hard to imagine she would ever have had this opportunity.

Long before becoming a vice president at Enron, Watkins showed signs of someone on the path to mastery. In high school she was a focused, diligent student and a member of the National Honor Society. When asked what motivated Watkins's pursuit of excellence, her mother pointed to her faith, saying, "Lutheran school always stressed that you do your best for the glory of God."[3] And Watkins clearly did her best in school and throughout her career. After graduating from high school, she earned a bachelor's degree in administration and a master's degree in accounting from the University of Texas at Austin— one of the top programs in the United States. This launched her career in accounting at the prestigious firm Arthur Andersen, where she excelled as an auditor for eight years. After some impressive stints on Wall Street, Watkins made her way back to Texas in 1993 to work for Enron, where for eight years she progressed rapidly up the org chart until she earned the title of vice president, reporting directly to the firm's CFO.[4]

With the benefit of hindsight, it's clear that all this experience was preparing Watkins for the experience and position of power she would need in order to help bring down one of the most corrupt corporations in American history. Jessica Uhl, a former Enron employee whom Watkins mentored, put it this way: "Sherron [had] a unique combination of skills, and that [made] her one of the best people in the company to [blow the whistle]. She [had] the background. She was a CPA, [she] worked at Arthur Andersen [the firm that audited Enron]. So she completely [got] what was going on in a way that other people might not."[5]

When I sat down to speak with Watkins, she was quick to point out that while it was important that she was excellent at the seemingly big things (having the right position within the company, knowing the latest accounting standards, and so on), it was equally important that she was excellent in the little things of her role—even something as ordinary as expense reports. Watkins explained, "When I was testifying before Congress, they showed me a document I had never seen before. It was a memo from Enron's outside law firm to Ken Lay, dated two days after my meeting with him. The subject of the memo was 'potential consequences to discharging employees who raise accounting concerns.' So Ken Lay's first action after our meeting was not to look into whether I spoke truth or not; it was to see if he could fire me without consequence. Now, I'm fairly certain that Enron looked through my expense reports to see if they could fire me for cause. At Enron, expense report abuse was fairly rampant. And when some manager or director or vice president would get crosswise with someone, they would often review their expense reports and find some discrepancy or sloppy work which would give them a reason to fire them for cause. And I never did that. I was always careful to take my time to do even the task of submitting expense reports rightly."[6]

Watkins later found out by speaking with other whistleblowers that often times the corrupt institution will work relentlessly to find some skeleton in the closet of the whistleblowing employee, using that as rationale to fire the employee, smear the employee's name, and destroy her credibility. "But I felt like I could take a stand and risk going to see Ken Lay because I didn't have any skeletons in my closet," Watkins said. "I hadn't booked any erroneous accounting entries, and I hadn't cheated on my expense reports. I tried my best to do every aspect of my work—even expense reports—with excellence, and I ended up being a very credible person."[7]

Even with her credibility intact, blowing the whistle on Enron took an incredible toll on Watkins. As soon as she discovered the fraud, Watkins started to interview for jobs at other corporations, knowing that the end of Enron was near. But after an experience like hers, Watkins couldn't help but question the meaning and significance of her work. "But thankfully, I had this very wise pastor who really changed my perspective," Watkins shared. "I remember him saying, 'Look, you've got these accounting skills, you've done well in your career, you are at the top of your field. You've been given these opportunities for a reason. Because of your position, you are serving as the Lord's eyes and ears in your field.'" Watkins realized her pastor was right. She said, "So many companies don't end up like Enron because there are faith-filled believers in positions of power within these firms, working to keep them on the right path."[8]

Watkins's story exemplifies the second promise of mastery: When we do our work with excellence—when we get truly masterful at our one thing—we are often put in positions of tremendous power. Proverbs 22:29 makes this promise explicit: "Do you see someone skilled in their work? They will serve before kings; they will not serve before officials of low rank." In the words of the hit musical *Hamilton,* mastery puts us in "the room where it happens"—where decisions are made, lives are changed, and power is palpable.

If the promise of power makes you a tad uncomfortable, you're not alone. Abuses of power are everywhere around us, and many in the church have responded to those abuses by tempering their ambition for fear of becoming power-mongering egomaniacs. But I don't believe this response is honoring to the Lord. Power can be a very good thing when it is viewed as a gift to be leveraged in service of others. Because Sherron Watkins was a master of her craft, she had the opportunity to serve in positions of great influence before the kings of her industry. But she didn't cling to or hoard that power. Rather, when she saw exploitation,

When we do our work with excellence—when we get truly masterful at our one thing—we are often put in positions of tremendous power.

she stepped up, took an enormous risk, and leveraged her power to stop it in order to accomplish the Lord's will and serve those around her.

Throughout the Bible we see similar examples of people who, because they were masters of their vocation, were placed in positions of great power in order to accomplish the Lord's will. Joseph was a masterful government leader who used his administrative skills to organize a massive hunger-relief program and save thousands of lives. Deborah's obedience and excellence as a judge led to forty years of peace for the Israelites and (we can assume) great honor and continued power for Deborah. Daniel so distinguished himself among the other administrators of Babylon that he was granted a high-ranking position under King Darius, causing the leader of the pagan empire to command his people to fear and revere Daniel's God.

Power is not inherently evil. Like everything else under the sun, power can and will be abused. But for those of us pursuing mastery of our chosen vocation, the promise of power should be incredibly motivating—not so that we can be seen as powerful or great, but so that we, like Joseph, Deborah, Daniel, and Watkins, can expend our power in service of others.

One of the most interesting biblical texts on this subject comes from Jesus's exchange with the disciples in Mark 10. To refresh your memory, here's the scene:

> Then James and John, the sons of Zebedee, came to [Jesus].
> "Teacher," they said, "we want you to do for us whatever
> we ask."
> "What do you want me to do for you?" he asked.
> They replied, "Let one of us sit at your right and the other
> at your left in your glory." (verses 35–37)

James and John were jockeying for power, shamelessly asking to sit on either side of the King of kings for all eternity. Not surprisingly, when the other ten disciples caught wind of this plea, they were irate. Mark said, "When the ten heard about this, they became indignant with James and John" (verse 41). The disciples were at each other's throats, squabbling about who would hold the position of highest honor, glory, and power in the kingdom of heaven. Then Jesus stepped in and cut through the clamor.

> Jesus called them together and said, "You know that those who
> are regarded as rulers of the Gentiles lord it over them, and their
> high officials exercise authority over them. Not so with you.
> Instead, whoever wants to become great among you must be
> your servant, and whoever wants to be first must be slave of all.
> For even the Son of Man did not come to be served, but to serve,
> and to give his life as a ransom for many." (verses 42–45)

I've long been fascinated with Jesus's words here, because while Jesus is clearly challenging the disciples' definition of greatness, he never reprimands them for their *desire* for greatness and power.* Why? I think it's because God is the one who put the desire for greatness in our hearts. Think back to the Garden of Eden. When God created humankind, he called them to "fill the earth and subdue it," to "rule over the fish in the sea and the birds in the sky, over the livestock and all the wild animals, and over all the creatures that move along the ground" (Genesis 1:26, 28). This is regal language. These are the duties of kings and queens. God wasn't calling Adam and Eve to "serve before officials of low rank" (Proverbs 22:29). He was granting humankind great power and responsibility. While sin has greatly distorted how we use power, our desire for it is hardwired into our DNA, placed there by the Creator himself.

Of course, Jesus knew this when he broke up this argument among the twelve disciples. If their desire for power was inherently bad, this exchange would have been the perfect opportunity for Jesus to say so. But he didn't. Instead, Jesus radically redefined what true power is. He said that, rather than using power to "lord it over" others, we should wield our power in service of others. Jesus is essentially saying, "You want to sit at the right hand of the King of kings? You want real power and true greatness? Stop focusing on being seen as great. Become a servant. Spend your power in service of others." Of course, soon after this discourse with the disciples, Jesus would live out the ultimate demonstration of this principle at Calvary. The King of kings—the perfect human being—would voluntarily empty himself of all his physical power in order to redeem the human race.

Jesus doesn't diminish our desire for power and greatness. He simply redirects it. This has incredible ramifications for us as we seek to

---

* Major shout-out to John Mark Comer for first pointing this out to me in his book, *Garden City*.

master our chosen vocations. Power isn't something we should shy away from; rather, we should lean fully and ambitiously into mastering the work the Lord has created us to do, accepting the power that comes along with it, not as a means of hoarding that influence for ourselves, but as a means of better loving and serving those around us.

It's important to recognize that "the room where it happens" isn't always a boardroom in which our power will impact tens of thousands of lives by bringing a behemoth enterprise crumbling to the ground. Sometimes, the room in which we leverage our power in service of others is relatively small. It may be a classroom, a cubicle, or a home. Regardless of the size of the room, mastery of our chosen one thing gives us power in these spaces to serve others.

> **Jesus doesn't diminish our desire for power and greatness. He simply redirects it.**

In chapter 5 I introduced you to Christy Adams, the masterful Spanish teacher who was first drawn to the idea of teaching language when she served as a translator on a missions trip to Mexico. Upon returning to the University of Georgia (UGA) after that trip, Adams felt called to volunteer to teach English as a second language to the Spanish-speaking immigrants in her community. It was then that her passion for what would become her one vocational thing really started to develop. When I asked Adams why she was so passionate about this work, she said, "I was just really moved by the plight of the immigrant. These were people who were marginalized in my community. They had bad experiences with English speakers. They were often treated poorly. And I saw teaching them the English language as the key to unlocking so much opportunity for them. It was quite literally a means of giving them a voice."

After graduating from UGA, Adams and her husband, Chris, moved to Gainesville, Georgia, where Christy secured her first full-time job teaching Spanish to English-speaking students, as well as English as a second language to the many Spanish speakers in the community. In many ways Gainesville was an ideal place for Adams to teach, given the large population of Spanish-speaking immigrants who worked at the massive chicken farms in that area.

Adams spent five years teaching language in the public school system before taking some time off to care for her firstborn child. But not long after the birth of her daughter, Adams was getting restless. "I knew I didn't want to go back to work full time just yet," Adams explained, "but I just felt angst over not using this gift of teaching that the Lord had called me to cultivate." Adams had seen firsthand how mastery leads to power. In her case she had seen her power as a masterful educator transform the lives of students in the classroom, and she missed leveraging her skills in that way. Adams was eager to put her skills back to work in service of others, even if it wasn't as a full-time teacher at her beloved school.

At the time, the Adamses attended church next to a run-down apartment complex with almost exclusively Spanish-speaking residents. "So one day, with my daughter in tow, I walked into the management office of this apartment complex and explained that I wanted to volunteer to teach an English class to the residents of the apartment complex," Adams explained. "And before I could launch into a whole long spiel, the manager tells me, 'If you want to start a class, you need to talk to Catalina.'"

Catalina (not her real name) was a lively woman who shared a small apartment with her husband and five kids. As the manager made clear, Catalina was also the unofficial mayor of the apartment complex. Adams shared, "So the manager took me to Catalina's door, I explained what I wanted to do, and she said, 'Oh, we're going to get a class all right. We're going to get a class together right now.'" Sure enough, Catalina and Adams went door to door and got more than twenty people together for that first session.

For the next two years, Adams faithfully leveraged her knowledge and power to teach these immigrants the English language, giving them the voice they needed to excel at work, at school, and in the community at large. Today, many members of that community are flourishing because Adams was willing to leverage her power as a master teacher on their behalf. When I asked how Catalina and her family were doing, Adams beamed with joy. "She and her family are doing really well. Her husband has a much better job. They've moved into a better home. And Catalina is learning even more English and teaching it to her now seven kids. She's even spending more time volunteering at her kids' schools because she now has the confidence that comes with language to be able to engage in the community in that way."

When the Adamses moved away from Gainesville two years after Catalina organized that first class, the residents of the apartment complex threw a surprise party for Christy and her family. "They were so sweet. They acted like my teaching them was such a huge deal," said Adams as she humbly demurred.[9]

But what Adams did *was* a huge deal. When you and I get masterful at our one thing, we will undoubtedly be granted greater and greater power, gaining access to rooms where that power can be leveraged in service of others, whether it's a boardroom or an apartment living room. This power is a good, God-given gift—not one that we should shy away from. Let us embrace the power that comes with mastery, not out of a desire for recognition but as a means to true greatness, pouring our power out in service of others.

Chapter Summary

The second promise of mastery is that when we do our work with excellence, we are often put in positions of power, which can be leveraged to accomplish the Lord's will. Power isn't something we should shy away from; rather, we should lean fully and ambitiously into mastering the work the Lord has created us to do, accepting the power that comes along with it, not as a means of hoarding that influence for ourselves, but as a means of better loving and serving those around us.

Key Scripture

"Do you see someone skilled in their work?
    They will serve before kings;
    they will not serve before officials of low rank" (Proverbs 22:29).

Next Action

Write down specific examples of how further mastery of your craft could earn you more power to expend sacrificially on behalf of others.

Chapter 11

Share the Master's Happiness

The climax of God's happiness is the delight
He takes in the echoes of His excellence.

JOHN PIPER

In the opening scene of the blockbuster hit *The Martian,* we are introduced to a group of hopeful astronauts living and working on Mars. But just a few minutes into the film, crisis strikes as the crew learns of an impending storm. Commander Lewis orders the crew to abort the mission, but as they are heading back to the shuttle, a satellite dish strikes astronaut Mark Watney, knocking him out of sight from his colleagues. The crew tries to find Watney, but the winds of the storm are so intense that the dust makes it impossible to see him. Convinced Watney is dead, the other astronauts board the shuttle without him, just in time to achieve liftoff and leave Mars. Watney miraculously survives, and throughout the rest of the movie, we witness his incredible fight for survival and rescue. But after more than a year of perseverance, Watney begins to lose hope that he will ever make it home. Sitting alone on the red planet, Watney types a message to Commander Lewis, asking her to deliver it to his parents in the event of his death. As he sits there searching for the words he wants his parents to hear, he says, "Please tell them, tell them I love what I do and I'm really good at it."[1]

Isn't that what we all want to be able to say about our work? "I love what I do and I'm really good at it." Nobody starts a career searching for work that they merely "like," "enjoy," or "tolerate." We all want to *love* our work. We all long for the joy that comes with finding the work we were created to do and becoming truly masterful at it.

But as we saw at the beginning of this book, you won't discover the work you love by following the conventional wisdom to "follow your passions" or "do whatever makes you happy." The truth—as established by scientists and the masters profiled throughout this book—is that there are serious flaws with the assumption that we will almost instantaneously find the vocational happiness we all long for if we focus primarily on finding work that aligns with a preexisting passion. As we have seen, passion, happiness, and the true satisfaction of vocation *follow* mastery, not the other way around. It is when we focus on the happiness of others and serving them well through excellent work that we find true vocational happiness for ourselves. It is only when we get insanely good at what we do that we don't just fall in love with our

> **It is only when we get insanely good at what we do that we don't just fall in love with our work but stay in love with it over a long period of time.**

work but stay in love with it over a long period of time. In the words of Mark Watney, we get to love what we do *by* getting really good at it. We find true vocational happiness for ourselves when we focus first on bringing joy to God and others by doing our work masterfully well.

But this others-first approach to our work doesn't mean we should suppress our desire to find work we love. As C. S. Lewis said, "The New Testament has lots to say about self-denial, but not about self-denial as an end in itself. We are told to deny ourselves and to take up our crosses in order that we may follow Christ; and nearly every description of what we shall ultimately find if we do so contains an appeal to desire."[2] In other words, our desire to find vocational happiness and work that we love is a good, God-honoring thing. John Piper put it this way: "The longing to be happy is a universal human experience, and it is good, not sinful. We should never try to deny or resist our longing to be happy, as though it were a bad impulse. Instead we should seek to intensify this longing and nourish it with whatever will provide the deepest and most enduring satisfaction. The deepest and most enduring happiness is found only in God. . . . The happiness we find in God reaches its consummation when it expands to meet the needs of others in the manifold ways of love."[3]

As we have explored in this book, hopping around from job to job and career to career—being a jack-of-all-trades and a master of none—may lead to moments of happiness in our work. But the path to finding the deepest and most enduring satisfaction of vocation is the path of mastery. To quote *Grit* author Angela Duckworth again, "Being a 'promising beginner' is fun, but being an actual expert is infinitely more gratifying." Why? Because mastery is how we, in the words of Piper, "meet the needs of others in the manifold ways of love" and get closer to our original design as image bearers of our exceptional God. We were not created for mediocrity. We were created for mastery. And when we pursue excellence in our work as a means of glorifying God and serving others, we are promised that we will share in the True Master's happiness for all eternity.

Jesus made this clear in one of his most famous parables, commonly known as the parable of the talents. In the story Jesus told of a master who, before setting out on a journey, entrusts his wealth to three servants. The master entrusts the first servant with five bags of gold, the second with two bags of gold, and the third with one bag. When the master returns from his trip, he learns that the third servant has lazily refused to invest the wealth the master has entrusted him with. When the master hears of this "wicked, lazy servant," he says, "Throw that worthless servant outside, into the darkness, where there will be weeping and gnashing of teeth" (Matthew 25:30). While the third servant was severely chastised by the master, the first two servants earned glowing praise for putting their talents to work and producing a 100 percent return on the master's money. To these two servants the master says, "Well done, good and faithful servant[s]! You have been faithful with a few things; I will put you in charge of many things. Come and share your master's happiness!" (Matthew 25:23).

Jesus's message in this parable couldn't be clearer: when we pursue mastery of the work God has created us to do, we are promised that we will share the Master's happiness. The pursuit of happiness in our work isn't a bad thing. Here, Jesus is clearly holding it out as an incentive and reward. But it is important to note that while the first two servants may have been motivated by their own happiness, Jesus doesn't tell us that in the parable. The servants' happiness is not the focal point of this story—the master's happiness is. Because the servants were focused first on pleasing their master, they were invited to share in the master's infinite happiness forever. As we've seen throughout this book, when we prioritize our own happiness in our work over service to others, we typically get neither. But when we focus on doing masterful work primarily for God's glory and the good of our neighbor, we bring joy to our Master, who graciously invites us to share in that happiness with him.

Like the three servants in Jesus's parable, all of us have been granted certain passions, gifts, and opportunities and have been called to make the most of them. In part 2 of this book, I sought to provide us with a guide for how to steward these gifts well, first by exploring our various vocational options, then by choosing to commit to mastering one and eliminating other work that would distract us from our essential mission, and finally by practicing the three keys to mastery. As the parable of the talents makes clear, the consequences for being poor stewards of the work the Father has given us to do are grim. But the promises of pursuing mastery of the work we were created to do couldn't be greater. As we have seen in this third and final part of the book, mastery in our work makes us the salt of the earth and the light of the world, it gives us access to power, and it opens the door for us to share in our Master's happiness—the greatest joy and happiness the world can ever know.

Many of us are far too content with the humdrum "happiness" that comes with being simply adequate at our work. We put up with just being okay at what we do, getting by with being mediocre, not leaning into what it takes to be masters of our craft and the very best stewards of the gifts and talents the Lord has given us. When we do this, we aren't just robbing God of the pleasure of seeing his children emulate his excellent image. We aren't just robbing the world of the contribution that we are uniquely positioned to make. When we fail to find, focus on, and master the work we were created to do, we rob ourselves of the deepest satisfaction of vocation. I think Lewis put this well when he said, "It would seem that Our Lord finds our desires not too strong, but too weak. We are half-hearted creatures, fooling about with drink and sex and ambition when infinite joy is offered us, like an ignorant child who wants to go on making mud pies in a slum because he cannot imagine what is meant by the offer of a holiday at the sea. We are far too easily pleased."[4]

Let us not be content with the shallow happiness that is so easily attained through mediocrity. Instead, let us passionately and unashamedly chase the infinite joy that comes with mastering the work we were created to do, thereby sharing the Master's happiness and feeling his pleasure.

While Eric Liddell was Scottish by blood, his heart was in China for nearly his entire life. Born in Tientsin, China, Liddell was the second son of Scottish missionaries who had dedicated their lives to sharing the gospel with the Chinese. From an early age Liddell expected to one day serve alongside his family as a missionary in China, but his parents required that he first attend boarding school in London. It was there that Liddell started to sense that God may have created him for work other than missions in China, for Liddell had discovered the joy of running. It didn't take long for those around Liddell to recognize his exceptional talents as a track and field athlete. By the time he enrolled at the University of Edinburgh, Liddell was known as the fastest runner in Scotland and had earned the nickname, the Flying Scotsman.

Liddell's story is perhaps most well-known as told by the Academy Award–winning movie *Chariots of Fire*. While the movie is primarily about the incredible true story of Liddell's competing in the 1924 Olympics, there's a compelling subplot that is quite pertinent to the subject of this book. Throughout the film we watch Liddell struggle with choosing whether to focus on missions work in China or his work as a star track athlete. Fortunately for Liddell the realities of geography forced him to choose just one thing to pour all his energy into at this particular stage of his life. There's a great scene early in the film when Liddell's family is on furlough, back home with their son in Scotland. While Liddell is weighing the choice he has to make, his father tells him, "You're a very lucky young man, Eric. You're the proud possessor of many gifts, and it's your sacred duty to put them to good use. Eric, you can praise the Lord by peeling a spud if you peel it to perfection. Don't compromise. Compromise is the language of the devil. Run in God's name, and let the world stand back in wonder."[5]

But while his father had given his blessing for Liddell to focus on mastering his work as a runner, Liddell's sister was less supportive, constantly pushing her brother to choose to focus on the missions work the family was doing in China. In another scene from *Chariots of Fire,* at the height of his sister's frustration, Liddell asks her to take a walk. As they stroll through the beautiful Scottish countryside, Liddell explains that in this season of his life, the work the Father had given him to do was not missions in China but running. His sister clearly doesn't understand, so Liddell patiently explains, "I believe that God . . . made me fast. And when I run, I feel his pleasure. To give that up would be to hold him in contempt. . . . To win is to honor him."[6]

The experience of feeling God's pleasure is one that came up in more than one interview with the masters profiled in this book, as individuals described the deep satisfaction of vocation that comes with being a master of one. But when I asked these masters to describe this experience, they struggled to put it into words. My mother-in-law, a children's choir director who has spent more than thirty years becoming truly world class at her craft, put it this way: "It's so hard to describe, but I know I have experienced moments in which I have said to myself, 'This is definitely it. *This* is the work God put me on earth to do.' But it's a really spiritual moment, so it's very difficult to describe in physical terms. But I think to feel God's pleasure is to take a step back from your work and know that the Lord is being honored and glorified by it. And that's what it's all about."[7]

Indeed, his glory and his pleasure *are* what it's all about. And to feel that pleasure as we pursue mastery of the work he created us to do is one of the greatest gifts imaginable. But what exactly does it look like to share in that happiness and feel God's pleasure? I think it looks like Eric Liddell's sense of satisfaction as he stood on the podium with a gold medal around his neck at the 1924 Olympics or when, nearly a century later, David Boudia stood on an Olympic podium in second place with his identity intact, satisfied that he honored the Lord by doing his one thing as masterfully as he knew how. I think it looks like C. S. Lewis and Antoni Gaudí having inexplicably brilliant creative breakthroughs that allowed them to tie their respective masterpieces together. I imagine Christy Adams feeling God's pleasure when she sits back in her chair at the end of the school year, knowing she is doing the work she was created to do, and Emily Ley experiencing the same thing when she ships her latest batch of planners to women around the world. I think the subtle smile on Tony Dungy's face when his team scored a touchdown is a pretty good picture of a master feeling God's pleasure, as are Scott Harrison's joyful tears as he watches a village get clean water for the very first time. I'm sure there were times Fred Rogers sensed God's pleasure when he was interacting with children in his Neighborhood of Make-Believe, a feeling similar to what Jessica Jones experiences when she does her job well and gets to watch a healthy newborn baby leave the NICU in her parents' arms. And as I write the final words of this book, I feel God's pleasure, knowing that I've done my one thing as exceptionally as I know how—not perfectly—but with the genuine pursuit of mastery of my craft as a means of serving you and honoring the One who has called me to this work.

> **We feel God's pleasure when we know we are doing the work he created us to do.**

We feel God's pleasure when we know we are doing the work he created us to do. We feel his pleasure when we do that work masterfully well. We feel his pleasure when we prioritize his happiness and his agenda over our own, committing ourselves to exceptional work for the glory of God and the good of others.

Everyone longs for work that brings great joy and happiness. Everyone yearns for the satisfaction of vocation. These desires are good things, etched onto our hearts by a good Father who longs to see his children experience great joy in their lives and in their work. As we've seen throughout this book, we don't find vocational joy by focusing primarily on our own happiness. We find the ultimate satisfaction of vocation when we prioritize the happiness of others over our own, when we pursue God's glory, rather than our own. And how do we glorify God and bring joy to others through our work? By doing the most exceptional work we know how. By embracing the truth of "less but better." By refusing to be content being a master of none, and instead choosing to be a master of one.

As we end this book, I pray that you would do what's necessary to find the work God has created you to do in this season of life. Then, once you've chosen that work, I pray that you would have the courage and discipline to focus intensely on that calling, pursuing mastery of your vocation so that you might bring God great glory, serve the world, and share in the Master's happiness forever.

Chapter Summary

The third and final promise of mastery is that when we pursue excellence in our work as a means of glorifying God and serving others, we are invited to share in the True Master's happiness. While our happiness is not the primary purpose of work, our desire to find work that we love is a good, God-honoring thing. The truest and deepest satisfaction of vocation *follows* mastery, not the other way around. It is only when we get insanely good at what we do that we not only fall in love with our work but stay in love with it over a long period of time.

Key Scripture

"Well done, good and faithful servant! . . . Come and share your master's happiness!" (Matthew 25:23).

Next Action

Before you close this book, spend a few minutes in prayer articulating to the Lord your commitment to masterful work for his happiness and the joy of others.

Acknowledgments

If you've never published a book, it can be difficult to appreciate just how many people contribute to a project of this magnitude. It literally took hundreds of people mastering their crafts and callings to get this book in your hands. A few of them deserve special acknowledgment here.

To Kara, my bride: This book is dedicated to you. Without your loving sacrifice, I wouldn't be able to pursue mastery of the work I believe I was created to do. Your gift of grace is appreciated more than you will ever know. I will love and cherish you as long as we both shall live.

To Chris Perry: There is no way this book would exist without you. While I was running a company full time, you forged ahead on this project and laid the groundwork with your masterful research. Thank you for being my chief collaborator on this project.

To the sources whose interviews make up this book: The biggest challenge in writing a book about focused, masterful work is that the people you want to interview are often too focused on their one thing to talk. I love and appreciate the irony! Still, many of you were generous with your schedules and offered ample time for me to plumb the depths of your wisdom. Thank you! Without you, this would be a very short, colorless book. Each of you deserve to be thanked by name: Brett Hagler, Christy Adams, Daniel Baltzer, Douglas Gresham, Jeff Heck, Jeremy Cowart, Jessica Jones, Joel Iverson, Josh Eicholtz, Dr. Junlei Li, Kelly Kannwischer, Mike Allen, Scott Kauffmann, Sheila Goskie, Sherron Watkins, Tony Dungy, and Wade Griffin.

To Tina Constable, Campbell Wharton, and Andrew Stoddard: Thank you for instantly grasping the vision for this book and betting on me. I'll never forget it.

To Ingrid Beck: You are truly masterful at your craft as an editor. Thank you for your rapid feedback and for pushing me to make this a much better book.

To Douglas Mann, Brett Benson, Pamela Shoup, and the rest of the team at WaterBrook and Penguin Random House: You all have made this an exceptional experience. Thank you for your commitment to the ministry of excellence. You are serving your authors well!

To D.J. Snell, Dana Ashley, Ian Crafford, and the entire team at Legacy Management: You guys are the dream team. I could not ask for better agents and partners in my endeavors.

To Jessica Penick and Jordan Wiseman: I am forever grateful for our partnership. Thank you for your commitment to helping us all engage with God's Word on a daily basis.

To my loyal tribe: Thank you for starting every Monday morning with me in your email inbox. Your enthusiasm for my content and constant encouragement means more to me than you will ever know. Thank you for allowing me to continue to serve you.

To the Launch Team: You all blew *Called to Create* out of the water, and while I am obviously writing this before *Master of One* hits bookstores, I have all the confidence in the world that we will do it together again with this title. Thank you for your energy, creativity, and enthusiasm for helping us all more deeply connect the gospel to our work.

To those who helped me develop the ideas for this book: Thank you! I badly needed conversations like the ones we had to flesh out my thinking on this project. Thank you for being willing collaborators!

Specifically, thanks to Brian Deming, Casey Cox, Chris Adams, Clay Brown, Erik Rapprich, Ian Salsman, Jennifer Banks, Jennifer Grashel, Jim O'Connell, Josh Finklea, Lee Stuart, Marcia Abramson, Meg Easterbrook, Payton Wetzel, Pat Wolff, Rick Mortensen, Rob Jelinski, Ryan Higgins, Sherryl LaPointe, Siyu Lin, Sloan Stuart, Terry Phong, Tony DeSisto, William Tarpeh, and William Warren.

To John Mark Comer, Greg McKeown, Tim Keller, Cal Newport, and Matt Perman: Your ideas and God's Word are the very foundation of this book. Thank you for paving the way for this work.

To the team at Threshold 360: Thank you for allowing me to pursue mastery of my one thing alongside you. You are exceptional at your respective crafts, and I am so glad we get to continue this journey together.

To The Church at Odessa: Nearly every Sunday, on the way home from worship, Kara and I verbalize how much we *love* our church family. We can't imagine a more wonderful place to call home. Thank you for your constant support of my family and my work. I hope we are half the blessing to you as you are to us.

To my Master: Thank you for the glorious gift of the gospel, which assures me that in either success or failure, you are good and I am loved.

Visit JordanRaynor.com to connect with
Jordan and discover additional resources
to help you master your one thing.

———

If you enjoyed this book, you will love
Jordan's national bestseller, *Called to Create*.
Available wherever books are sold.

Notes

Introduction

1. Anders Ericsson and Robert Pool, *Peak: Secrets from the New Science of Expertise* (Boston: Houghton Mifflin Harcourt, 2016), 109.

2. "How Millennials Want to Work and Live," Gallup, 2016, www.gallup.com/workplace/238073/millennials-work-live.aspx.

3. Heather Long, "The New Normal: 4 Job Changes by the Time You're 32," CNN Business, April 12, 2016, https://money.cnn.com/2016/04/12/news/economy/millennials-change-jobs-frequently/index.html.

4. Patrick Gillespie, "Intuit: Gig Economy Is 34% of US Workforce," CNN, May 24, 2017, https://money.cnn.com/2017/05/24/news/economy/gig-economy-intuit/index.html.

5. Greg McKeown, *Essentialism: The Disciplined Pursuit of Less* (New York: Crown Business, 2014), 3.

6. Andreas J. Köstenberger, *Excellence: The Character of God and the Pursuit of Scholarly Virtue* (Wheaton, IL: Crossway, 2011), 36.

7. John Piper, *Don't Waste Your Life, Group Study Edition* (Wheaton, IL: Crossway, 2007), 31.

8. Köstenberger, *Excellence*, 43.

9. McKeown, *Essentialism*, 9.

10. John Mark Comer, *Garden City: Work, Rest, and the Art of Being Human* (Grand Rapids, MI: Zondervan, 2015), 135. Copyright ©

2015 by John Mark Comer. Used by permission of Zondervan. www.zondervan.com.

11. McKeown, *Essentialism,* 124.

12. Timothy Keller, "With the Anxious," The Real Jesus sermon series, February 9, 1997.

Chapter 1: Excellence in All Things

1. "The Big Win (Excellence—Chapter 1)," FCA Resources: Devotional, December 1, 2008, http://fcaresources.com/devotional/big -win-excellence-chapter-1.

2. "The Big Win."

3. Marvin Harrison, "Enshrinement Speech," delivered on August 6, 2016, at Tom Benson Hall of Fame Stadium in Canton, OH, www.profootballhof.com/players/marvin-harrison/.

4. "The Big Win."

5. Albert Mohler, " 'Excellence in All Things and All Things to God's Glory'—The Legacy of Dr. D. James Kennedy," AlbertMohler .com, September 5, 2007, https://albertmohler.com/2007/09/05 /excellence-in-all-things-and-all-things-to-gods-glory-the-legacy -of-dr-d-james-kennedy/.

6. John Piper, "Glorifying God . . . Period," DesiringGod.org, July 15, 2013, www.desiringgod.org/messages/glorifying-god -period.

7. John Mark Comer, *Garden City: Work, Rest, and the Art of Being Human* (Grand Rapids, MI: Zondervan, 2015), Kindle edition, 80. Used by permission of Zondervan. www.zondervan.com.

8. Comer, *Garden City,* 145.

9. Comer, *Garden City,* 74.

10. Comer, *Garden City*, 145.

11. Greg McKeown, *Essentialism: The Disciplined Pursuit of Less* (New York: Crown Business, 2014), 15.

12. John Naish, "Is Multi-Tasking Bad for Your Brain? Experts Reveal the Hidden Perils of Juggling Too Many Jobs," *Daily Mail*, August 11, 2009, www.dailymail.co.uk/health/article-1205669/Is-multi -tasking-bad-brain-Experts-reveal-hidden-perils-juggling-jobs.html.

13. Fred Shapiro and Barry Popik, "Put All Your Eggs in One Basket, and Then Watch That Basket," Quote Investigator.com, February 16, 2017, https://quoteinvestigator.com/2017/02/16/eggs/.

14. Cal Newport, *So Good They Can't Ignore You: Why Skills Trump Passion in the Quest for Work You Love* (New York: Grand Central, 2012), Kindle edition, chapter 1.

15. Newport, *So Good*, chapter 2.

16. Newport, *So Good*, chapter 3.

17. "Workplace Wellness," Mental Health America, www.mentalhealth america.net/workplace-wellness.

18. John Piper, *Desiring God: Meditations of a Christian Hedonist*, rev. ed. (Colorado Springs, CO: Multnomah, 2011), 28.

Chapter 2: Proclaiming the Excellencies of God

1. "Most Visited Tourist Attractions in the City of Barcelona in 2016 (in 1,000 visitors)," Statista, www.statista.com/statistics/457335 /barcelona-s-most-visited-tourist-attractions-spain/.

2. "History of the Basílica," Basílica de la Sagrada Família, www .sagradafamilia.org/en/history-of-the-temple/.

3. Giles Fraser, "Barcelona's Sagrada Família: Gaudí's 'Cathedral for the Poor'—A History of Cities in 50 Buildings, Day 49," *Guardian*,

June 3, 2015, www.theguardian.com/cities/2015/jun/03/barcelona
-sagrada-familia-gaudi-history-cities-cathedral- poor-church
-religion.

4. Jonathan Glancey, "Gaudí's Unfinished Sagrada Família Does Not
Need a Completion Date," *Guardian,* September 23, 2011, www
.theguardian.com/commentisfree/2011/sep/23/gaudi-sagrada
-familia.

5. Fraser, "Barcelona's Sagrada Família."

6. "Antoni Gaudí," Wikipedia, https://en.wikipedia.org/wiki/Antoni
_Gaud%C3%AD.

7. Andreas J. Köstenberger, *Excellence: The Character of God and the
Pursuit of Scholarly Virtue* (Wheaton, IL: Crossway, 2011), 33–34.

8. Dorothy Sayers, "Why Work?" TNL Church, http://tnl.org/wp
-content/uploads/Why-Work-Dorothy-Sayers.pdf.

9. Köstenberger, *Excellence,* 36–41.

10. David Boudia, *Greater Than Gold: From Olympic Heartbreak to
Ultimate Redemption* (Nashville, TN: Nelson, 2016), 57–58. Taken
from *Greater Than Gold* by David Boudia. Copyright © 2016 by
David Boudia. Used by permission of Thomas Nelson. www.thomas
nelson.com.

11. Boudia, *Greater Than Gold,* 10.

12. Boudia, *Greater Than Gold,* viii.

13. Boudia, *Greater Than Gold,* 15.

14. Boudia, *Greater Than Gold,* 58.

15. Boudia, *Greater Than Gold,* 82.

16. Boudia, *Greater Than Gold,* 85.

17. Boudia, *Greater Than Gold,* 100.

18. Boudia, *Greater Than Gold,* 100.

19. Boudia, *Greater Than Gold,* 101.

20. "David Boudia & Steele Johnson—Faith Statement," Victory Lutheran Church, Mesa, AZ, Vimeo video, August 15, 2016, https://vimeo.com/178956277.

21. Boudia, *Greater Than Gold,* 122.

Chapter 3: The Ministry of Excellence

1. Jessica Jones, phone interview with the author on July 27, 2018.

2. Matthew Aaron Perman, *What's Best Next: How the Gospel Transforms the Way You Get Things Done* (Grand Rapids, MI: Zondervan, 2016), Kindle edition.

3. Timothy Keller, *Every Good Endeavor: Connecting Your Work to God's Work* (New York: Penguin, 2012), 76.

4. John Mark Comer, *Garden City: Work, Rest, and the Art of Being Human* (Grand Rapids, MI: Zondervan, 2015), Kindle Edition. Used by permission of Zondervan. www.zondervan.com.

5. Tom Goldman, "New Dallas Mavericks CEO Has a Big Job Ahead of Her," NPR, May 22, 2018, www.npr.org/2018/05/22/613254314/new-dallas-mavericks-ceo-has-a-big-job-ahead-of-her.

6. Jon Wertheim and Jessica Luther, "Exclusive: Inside the Corrosive Workplace Culture of the Dallas Mavericks," *Sports Illustrated,* February 20, 2018, www.si.com/nba/2018/02/20/dallas-mavericks-sexual-misconduct-investigation-mark-cuban-response.

7. Eddie Sefko and Karen Robinson-Jacobs, "She Beat Cancer, Domestic Abuse and Racial Barriers, But Can She Save the Dallas Mavericks?" *Dallas News,* SportsDay, March 26, 2018, https://sportsday.dallasnews.com/dallas-mavericks/mavericks/2018/05/17/meet-woman-will-try-save-dallas-mavericks.

8. "Knocked Down But Never Out: Cynt Marshall Shares Her Amazing Story," AT&T, April 30, 2015, YouTube video, www.you tube.com/watch?v=bP9wcOZZ5GE.

9. "Knocked Down But Never Out."

10. "GEA: Cynthia Marshall Speech," TDH Media, filmed at the 2012 Guilford Education Alliance: Education Summit, January 2, 2013, YouTube video, https://youtube.com/watch?v=w7lK31wIAj8.

11. Goldman, "New Dallas Mavericks CEO."

12. "Game Changers: Cynthia Marshall," *L. A. Focus,* June 5, 2018, http://lafocusnewspaper.com/top-stories/item/game-changers -cynthia-marshall.

13. Goldman, "New Dallas Mavericks CEO."

14. Caroline Clarke, "Meet The Dallas Mavericks' New CEO," *Black Enterprise,* February 26, 2018, http://blackenterprise.com/mark -cuban-will-woman-take-mavericks-ceo/.

15. Deborah Ferguson, "Dallas Mavericks CEO Launches 100-Day Plan in Wake of Scandal," NBCDFW, April 2, 2018, http://nbcdfw .com/news/sports/Dallas-Mavericks-CEO-Launches-100-Day -Plan-After-Scandal--478542193.html.

Chapter 4: Start with "The One" in Mind

1. Douglas Gresham, phone interview with the author on June 20, 2018.

2. Angela Duckworth, *Grit: The Power of Passion and Perseverance* (New York: Scribner, 2016), Kindle edition, 87.

3. "I Am Moana (Song of the Ancestors)," music and lyrics by Lin-Manuel Miranda, Mark Mancina, and Opetaia Foa'i, performed by Auli'i Cravalho and Rachel House, release date November 18, 2016.

4. *Moneyball,* directed by Bennett Miller (Los Angeles: Columbia Pictures, 2011).

5. Andy Crouch, *Culture Making: Recovering Our Creative Calling* (Downers Grove, IL: InterVarsity, 2009), 253.

6. Crouch, *Culture Making,* 254.

7. Crouch, *Culture Making,* 256.

8. Crouch, *Culture Making,* 256.

Chapter 5: Explore

1. Emily Ley, *Grace, Not Perfection (with Bonus Content): Celebrating Simplicity, Embracing Joy* (Nashville, TN: Thomas Nelson, 2016), 139. Taken from *Grace, Not Perfection* by Emily Ley. Copyright © 2016 by Emily Ley. Used by permission of Thomas Nelson. www.thomasnelson.com.

2. Anna James, "Ladies Who Laptop: Chatting with Emily Ley of The Simplified Planner," *Lauren Conrad* (blog), June 17, 2015, https://laurenconrad.com/blog/2015/06/ladies-who-laptop-chatting-with-emily-ley-of-the-simplified-planner/.

3. Ley, *Grace, Not Perfection,* 163.

4. Ley, *Grace, Not Perfection,* 164.

5. Ley, *Grace, Not Perfection,* 164.

6. Ley, *Grace, Not Perfection,* 164.

7. Ley, *Grace, Not Perfection,* 168.

8. Ley, *Grace, Not Perfection,* 169.

9. Greg McKeown, *Essentialism: The Disciplined Pursuit of Less* (New York: Crown Business, 2014), 60.

10. Christy Adams, interview with the author on July 26, 2018.

11. Adams, interview.

12. Angela Duckworth, *Grit: The Power of Passion and Perseverance* (New York: Scribner, 2016), 104.

13. Matthew Aaron Perman, *What's Best Next: How the Gospel Transforms the Way You Get Things Done* (Grand Rapids, MI: Zondervan, 2016), Kindle edition.

14. Jeff Heck, phone interview with the author on June 27, 2018.

Chapter 6: Choose

1. Maxwell King, *The Good Neighbor: The Life and Work of Fred Rogers* (New York: Abrams, 2019), 117.

2. Dr. Junlei Li, phone interview with the author on September 7, 2018.

3. King, *The Good Neighbor,* 10.

4. King, *The Good Neighbor,* 337.

5. King, *The Good Neighbor,* 116.

6. King, *The Good Neighbor,* 51.

7. King, *The Good Neighbor,* 58.

8. King, *The Good Neighbor,* 48.

9. King, *The Good Neighbor,* 67.

10. Ree Hines, "Mister Rogers 'Hated' TV—So 48 Years Ago, He Changed It," *Today,* August 30, 2016, www.today.com /parents/mister-rogers-hated-tv-so-48-years-ago-he-changed -t102349.

11. King, *The Good Neighbor,* 68.

12. King, *The Good Neighbor,* 68.

13. King, *The Good Neighbor,* 327.

14. Eric Ries, *The Lean Startup: How Today's Entrepreneurs Use Continuous Innovation to Create Radically Successful Businesses* (New York: Currency, 2011), 149.

15. John Mark Comer, *Garden City: Work, Rest, and the Art of Being Human* (Grand Rapids, MI: Zondervan, 2015), Kindle edition. Copyright © 2015 by John Mark Comer. Used by permission of Zondervan. www.zondervan.com.

16. Robert Greene, *Mastery* (New York: Penguin, 2012), 40.

17. Josh Eicholtz, phone interview with the author on August 4, 2018.

18. Barry Schwartz, *The Paradox of Choice: Why More Is Less* (New York: Harper Collins, 2003).

19. Charlie Rose, "Hamilton," *60 Minutes,* November 8, 2015, www .cbsnews.com/news/hamilton-broadway-musical-60-minutes-charlie -rose/.

20. J. Hampton Keathley, III, "Mark #11: The Pursuit of Excellence," Bible.org, May 26, 2004, https://bible.org/seriespage/mark-11 -pursuit-excellence.

21. "Scott's story," charity: water, https://my.charitywater.org/about /scott-harrison-story.

22. Scott Harrison, *Thirst: A Story of Redemption, Compassion, and a Mission to Bring Clean Water to the World* (New York: Currency, 2018), 62.

23. Harrison, *Thirst,* 109.

24. Harrison, *Thirst,* 140.

25. Harrison, *Thirst,* 141.

26. Harrison, *Thirst,* 141.

27. charity: water, www.charitywater.org/.

Chapter 7: Eliminate

1. Emily Ley, *Grace, Not Perfection (with Bonus Content): Celebrating Simplicity, Embracing Joy* (Nashville, TN: Thomas Nelson, 2016),

11. Taken from *Grace, Not Perfection* by Emily Ley. Copyright ©
2016 by Emily Ley. Used by permission of Thomas Nelson. www
.thomasnelson.com.

2. Ley, *Grace, Not Perfection,* 39.

3. Ley, *Grace, Not Perfection,* 61.

4. Timothy Keller, *Jesus the King: Understanding the Life and Death
of the Son of God* (New York: Penguin, 2016), 7–8.

5. John Mark Comer, *Garden City: Work, Rest, and the Art of Being
Human* (Grand Rapids, MI: Zondervan, 2015), Kindle edition.
Copyright © 2015 by John Mark Comer. Used by permission of
Zondervan. www.zondervan.com.

6. Greg McKeown, *Essentialism: The Disciplined Pursuit of Less* (New
York: Crown Business, 2014), 23.

7. Ryan Holiday, *Perennial Seller: The Art of Making and Marketing
Work That Lasts* (New York: Penguin, 2017), Kindle edition,
127.

8. "CPA Exam," Professional Training, *Washington Post,* www
.washingtonpost.com/wp-adv/eduadv/kaplan/kart_prof_meetexam
.html.

9. Chip Gaines, *Capital Gaines: Smart Things I Learned Doing Stupid
Stuff* (Nashville, TN: Thomas Nelson, 2017), 134.

10. Gaines, *Capital Gaines,* 134.

11. Gaines, *Capital Gaines,* 134.

12. Gaines, *Capital Gaines,* 136, 139.

13. Gaines, *Capital Gaines,* 129–30.

Chapter 8: Master

1. Dictionary.com, s.v. "Apprentice," www.dictionary.com/browse
/apprenticeship.

2. Emily Ley, *Grace, Not Perfection (with Bonus Content): Celebrating Simplicity, Embracing Joy* (Nashville, TN: Thomas Nelson, 2016), 168. Taken from *Grace, Not Perfection* by Emily Ley. Copyright © 2016 by Emily Ley. Used by permission of Thomas Nelson. www .thomasnelson.com.

3. Robert Greene, *Mastery* (New York: Penguin, 2012), 102.

4. Greene, *Mastery*, 93.

5. Maxwell King, *The Good Neighbor: The Life and Work of Fred Rogers* (New York: Abrams, 2018), Kindle edition.

6. Scott Harrison, *Thirst: A Story of Redemption, Compassion, and a Mission to Bring Clean Water to the World* (New York: Currency, 2018), 218.

7. Harrison, *Thirst*, 220.

8. Harrison, *Thirst*, 220.

9. Harrison, *Thirst*, 221.

10. Harrison, *Thirst*, 223.

11. Harrison, *Thirst*, 221.

12. Harrison, *Thirst*, 254.

13. Joshua Foer, *Moonwalking with Einstein: The Art and Science of Remembering Everything* (New York: Penguin, 2011), Kindle edition.

14. Ben Carter, "Can 10,000 Hours of Practice Make You an Expert?" BBC, March 1, 2014, www.bbc.com/news/magazine-26384712.

15. K. Anders Ericsson, Ralf Th. Krampe, and Clemens Tesch-Römer, "The Role of Deliberate Practice in the Acquisition of Expert Performance," *Psychological Review*, 100, no. 3, (1993): 1, http:// projects.ict.usc.edu/itw/gel/EricssonDeliberatePracticePR93.pdf.

16. Malcom Gladwell, *Outliers: The Story of Success* (Boston: Little, Brown and Company, 2008), 41.

17. Anders Ericsson and Robert Pool, *Peak: Secrets from the New Science of Expertise* (Boston: Houghton Mifflin Harcourt, 2016), 14–15.

18. Ericsson and Pool, *Peak,* 14.

19. Angela Duckworth, *Grit: The Power of Passion and Perseverance* (New York: Scribner, 2016), 121.

20. Ericsson and Pool, *Peak,* 15.

21. Duckworth, *Grit,* 122.

22. Ericsson and Pool, *Peak,* 17.

23. Duckworth, *Grit,* 121.

24. Duckworth, *Grit,* 58.

25. Duckworth, *Grit,* 87.

26. Duckworth, *Grit,* 54.

27. Jeff Heck, phone interview with the author on June 27, 2018.

Chapter 9: Salt and Light

1. Andy Crouch, *Culture Making: Recovering Our Creative Calling* (Downers Grove, IL: InterVarsity, 2009), 69.

2. David A. Price, *The Pixar Touch: The Making of a Company* (New York: Random House, 2008), 210.

3. Emma Green, "Lecrae: 'Christians Have Prostituted Art to Give Answers,'" *Atlantic,* October 6, 2014, www.theatlantic.com /entertainment/archive/2014/10/lecrae-christians-have-prostituted -art-to-give-answers/381103/.

4. Timothy Keller, "The Bible on Church and Culture," *Timothy Keller* (blog) April 1, 2008, http://timothykeller.com/blog/2008/4/1 /the-bible-on-church-and-culture.

5. Green, "Lecrae."

6. Douglas Gresham, phone interview with the author on June 20, 2018.

7. Gresham, interview.

8. Gresham, interview.

9. Wade Griffin, interview with the author on July 5, 2018.

10. Tony Dungy, interview with the author on October 29, 2018.

11. Dungy, interview.

12. "Peyton Manning's First Super Bowl Ring!, Colts vs. Bears Super Bowl XLI, NFL Full Game," NFL, published August 5, 2016, YouTube video, Tony Dungy speech at 2:28:18, www.youtube.com /watch?v=pAsarBgakuc.

13. Dungy, interview.

14. "Event Statistics," SXSW, April 19, 2018, https://explore.sxsw .com/hubfs/Hosted%20Files/2018-SXSW-Event-Stats-April-2018 .pdf.

15. Mike Murphy, "You Can Now 3D-Print a House in Under a Day," *Quartz,* March 12, 2018, https://qz.com/1227301/sxsw-2018 -affordable-3d-printed-houses-from-icon-and-charity-new-story -debuted-in-austin/.

16. Brett Hagler, phone interview with the author on June 22, 2018.

Chapter 10: *The Room Where It Happens*

1. Ted Barrett, "Enron CEO Warned About 'Wave of Accounting Scandals,'" CNN, January 14, 2002, www.cnn.com/2002/LAW /01/14/enron.letter/.

2. Richard Lacayo and Amanda Ripley, "Persons of the Year 2002: The Whistleblowers," *Time,* December 30, 2002, http://content.time .com/time/subscriber/printout/0,8816,1003998,00.html.

3. Jennifer Frey, "The Woman Who Saw Red," *Washington Post,* January 25, 2002, www.washingtonpost.com/archive/lifestyle /2002/01/25/the-woman-who-saw-red/8069b058-272c-45b7 -ad94-740f227e4706/?noredirect=on&utm_term=.ce217acb66e4.

4. Archives, "Text of Watkins' Testimony at House Hearing on Enron," *New York Times,* February 14, 2002, www.nytimes .com/2002/02/14/business/text-of-watkins-testimony-at-house-hearing-on-enron.html.

5. Frey, "The Woman Who Saw Red."

6. Sherron Watkins, phone interview with the author on June 25, 2018.

7. Watkins, interview.

8. Watkins, interview.

9. Christy Adams, interview with the author on July 26, 2018.

Chapter 11: Share the Master's Happiness

1. *The Martian,* directed by Ridley Scott (Los Angeles: Twentieth Century Fox, 2015).

2. C. S. Lewis, *The Weight of Glory* (New York: Harper Collins, 2009), 25–26.

3. John Piper, *Desiring God: Meditations of a Christian Hedonist,* rev. ed. (Colorado Springs, CO: Multnomah, 2011), 28.

4. Lewis, *The Weight of Glory,* 26.

5. *Chariots of Fire,* directed by Hugh Hudson, Twentieth Century Fox, 1981.

6. *Chariots of Fire,* 1981.

7. Sheila Goskie, interview with the author on August 31, 2018.